Revisiting W.B. Yeats's World and Art

Edited by

Bijay Kumar Das

ATLANTIC
PUBLISHERS & DISTRIBUTORS (P) LTD

Published by
ATLANTIC
PUBLISHERS & DISTRIBUTORS (P) LTD

7/22, Ansari Road, Darya Ganj, New Delhi-110002
Phones : +91-11-40775252, 23273880, 23275880, 23280451
Fax : +91-11-23285873
Web : www.atlanticbooks.com
E-mail : orders@atlanticbooks.com

Branch Office
5, Nallathambi Street, Wallajah Road, Chennai-600002
Phones : +91-44-64611085, 32413319
E-mail : chennai@atlanticbooks.com

Printed in India at Nice Printing Press, A-33/3A, Site-IV, Industrial Area, Sahibabad, Ghaziabad, U.P.

In memory
of
Balchandra Rajan,
Who paved the way

Preface

It is a paradox that the two greatest poets of English literature in the twentieth century, Yeats and Eliot, came from outside the English tradition. They have many things in common, that is, both of them dealt with personality and impersonality in their poetry. Again, both of them created personal myths and symbols in their poetry. When Eliot excels in long poems, Yeats shines in short lyrics. This book is occasioned by the one hundred fiftieth birth anniversary of W.B. Yeats.

Western critics have examined Yeats's poetry thoroughly from almost all angles. We can't add anything new to it using Western ideas and criticism. Therefore, an attempt has been made to understand Yeats *vis-à-vis* an American canonical author, Henry David Thoreau, from the standpoint of Indian poetics, though some of the papers included here have used Western ideas and criticism. I have raised two points which need further research by the Westerners as well as the Indians. They are, what exactly was the Yeats-Maud Gonne relationship? If it was love, what kind of love was that? Freudian or Lacanian? The second point is that if Yeats could get Nobel Prize for Literature in 1923, before his very best *The Tower* volume of poems was published, should we take that the Nobel Committee failed to anticipate the emergence of Yeats as a modern poet? If not, surely Yeats deserved another Nobel Prize.

Yeats has both inspired and influenced generations of poets and writers in the English speaking world, including two best known Indian English poets, Nissim Ezekiel and A.K. Ramanujan. The book is a tribute to Yeats from India as a token of love and admiration for him. And it is dedicated to Balchandra Rajan, the best critic on Yeats from India.

I would like to thank Atlantic Publishers & Distributors (P) Ltd., particularly the Chairman Dr. K.R. Gupta for bringing out the book in record time.

Bijay Kumar Das

Contents

Preface .... *v*

Contributors .... *ix*

1. Introduction 1
Bijay Kumar Das

2. Yeats's Response to Thoreau: Appropriations, Assimilations, Parallels and Convergences 6
R.W. Desai

3. Yeats, the Poet's Quarrel with Himself 26
S. Viswanathan

4. Yeats's Journey from 'Byzantium' to 'Meru' 35
S. Ramaswamy

5. 'A Woman Lost': A Reading of the Maud Gonne Poems of Yeats 42
C.T. Indra

6. The Poetry of Unageing Intellect 56
Prabhat K. Singh

7. A Note on Yeats's Poetry 66
Mohan Ramanan

8. Politics, Drama and Poetry: The Political Vision of W.B. Yeats as Reflected in Selected "Political" Plays and Poems 73
Prashant K. Sinha

9. *Dhvani* Theory and the Poetry of W.B. Yeats 89
Haladhar Panda

10. Reconfiguring the Poet and the Humanist in W.B. Yeats's Poetry 102
Bijay Kumar Das

11. The Personal and the Impersonal: Yeats Versus Eliot 113
Rajnath

Select Bibliography 122

Index 124

Contributors

Bijay Kumar Das: Professor of English, the University of Burdwan, Burdwan (West Bengal).

R.W. Desai: Former Professor of English, University of Delhi, Delhi and author of *Yeats's Shakespeare* (1971).

S. Viswanathan: Former Professor of English, University of Hyderabad, Hyderabad.

S. Ramaswamy: Formerly on the Faculty of English, Bangalore University and Fellow, Silliman College, Yale University.

C.T. Indra: Former Professor of English, Madras University, Chennai.

Prabhat K. Singh: Former Professor of English, Mahatma Gandhi Kashi Vidyapith, Varanasi.

Mohan Ramanan: Former Professor of English, University of Hyderabad, Hyderabad.

Prasanta K. Sinha: Former Professor of English, Poona University, Pune.

Haladhar Panda: Former Professor of English, Sambalpur University, Sambalpur (Odisha).

Rajnath: Former Professor of English, the University of Allahabad, Allahabad.

1

Introduction

Bijay Kumar Das

William Butler Yeats (1865-1939) has placed all of us—the Indians in his debt by encouraging Rabindranath Tagore to translate his *Gitanjali* into English which brought the latter Nobel Prize for Literature for 1913. It needs to be reiterated that Tagore is the only Indian to win this coveted prize in the last 102 years. That makes us all the more grateful to pay tribute to this great poet, W.B. Yeats in his one hundred and fiftieth year of his birth, this year (i.e., 2015). Yeats has been read, eulogized, evaluated and adored in the last one hundred years by critics of all hues—from traditional to postcolonial across the globe. A. Norman Jeffares, Richard Ellmann, T.R. Henn, T.S. Eliot, F.R. Leavis, Ezra Pound, Frank Kermode, Harold Bloom, C.K. Stead, W.H. Auden, Thomas Kinsella, B. Rajan, Terence Brown and Edward Said are some of the leading critics on W.B. Yeats who have taught us how to read W.B. Yeats for the last one hundred years, and set the taste for the age.

Let me begin with Richard Ellmann's significant observation on Yeats as a poet and a man:

> He looked the poet, and he lived the poet. He has justified and reinforced everything by autobiography, essay and public speech, has written the history of the movements that he joined or began and the biographies of his friends to bring all into coherence, nothing is left to chance. (*Yeats: The Man and the Mask* 1979)

Critics have described Yeats variously as a romantic, nationalist, symbolist, and above all an Irish poet. All these labels stuck over the years. But Yeats had outgrown all these labels with the arrival of later critics on the critical scene. For instance, Edward Said has tried his best to depict Yeats as a postcolonial poet in an essay called "Yeats and Decolonialism" (1988). What is remarkable about Yeats is that he is a genuine poet of the old age. His poetry abounds in binaries such as youth and age, art and life, mortality and immortality, transience and permanence.

Love, death and old age are recurrent themes in Yeats's poetry. Women play a vital role in Yeats's life as well as poetry. Love is the central theme in his poetry and Maud Gonne becomes the nerve centre as Yeats 'cast his heart into rhymes'. Consummation of love and the desire to be united with Maud Gonne became an obsession with Yeats, who said, "O that I were young again/ And held her in my arms".

Other kinds of love follow suit. Irish legend, folklore and mythology remain an integral part of Yeats's poetry. Yeats looked up to Irish mythology for themes. The sustained development in Yeats's poetry is due to the poet's shifting stance from the personal to the impersonal, from the man to the country (should we say, nation?). From Celtic movement to Irish folklore and then from Oriental Vision to Irish nation, Yeats's poetry stands exquisitely balanced. As he approached his death in 1939, Yeats emphasized his Irishness and sense of belonging to Irland in his last poems such as "The Municipal Gallery Revisited" (1937), "Under Ben Bulben" (1938) and "The Circle Animals' Desertion". He implored upon the Irish poets to understand the art of writing poetry in the following lines in "Under Ben Bulben":

> Irish poets, learn your trade,
> Sing, whatever is well made.

Yeats longed for writing about his race and country in "The Fisherman". He wrote:

> What I had hoped 't would be
> To write for my own race
> And the reality,
> The living men that I hate
> The Deadman that I loved....

Yeats had inwardness with human nature. He knew the difference between writing about a man when he was alive and when he is dead.

The circus animals, "Lion and Woman and the Lord Knows What" derived from folklore, history, literature and may be, theosophy remind Yeats of this past, "We Irish, born into that ancient sect" ("The Statues"). Yeats becomes conscious of the tradition and thanks all who contribute to it in "The Muncipal Gallery Revisited".

> Ireland's history in their lineament trace;
> Think where man's glory most begins and ends,
> And say my glory was I had such friends.

Here I am reminded of Yeats's letter to Dorothy Wellesley about Olivia Shakespear's death (three months and a half before his own death) in which he stated that, "for more than forty years she has been the centre of my life in London and during all that time we have never had a quarrel, sadness sometimes but never a difference...I will find her memory everywhere" (qtd. in *Yeats: Collection of Critical Essays* edited by John Unterecker 28). Yeats never lived in Ireland permanently till the establishment of the Free State in 1922 and therefore, his prolonged stay in London brought him closer to many people there and helped him to develop an inwardness with English literature. R.W. Desai's well-researched book, *Yeats's Shakespeare* brings home the point of Yeats's interaction with Shakespearean texts.

Before concluding my "Introduction", I would like to say a few words about the articles included in this book.

The book contains ten papers, apart from "Introduction" by the Editor. R.W. Desai's well-researched paper, "Yeats's Response to Thoreau: Appropriations, Assimilations, Parallels and Convergences" sets the tone of the book. Desai examines Yeats's letters, Thoreau's *Walden* and particularly Thoreau-Ellen Sewall love relationship to drive home the enigmatic Yeats-Maud Gonne affair. Desai's research supervisor Richard Ellmann provided him a context in *Golden Codgers: Biographical Speculations* to explore parallels, appropriations and convergences between the two all time great authors Thoreau and Yeats. Desai has explicated Yeats's "The Wild Swan at Coole" to find echoes of Thoreau's "Spring" in *Walden*. Lines from both the authors were examined with insight and precision in course of the paper leading to Desai's conclusion "the convergences between Yeats and Thoreau's thought are too close to be dismissed as coincidental".

S. Viswanathan's paper, "Yeats, the Poet's Quarrel with Himself" deals with Yeats's connection with India through Mohini Chatterjee and Sri Purohit Swami. He finds Yeats's personality dramatized in his poetry. To him Yeats is not merely a Romantic but a Modernist. There is a fusion of the Romantic and Modernity in his poetry.

S. Ramaswamy's paper, "Yeats's Journey from 'Byzantium' to 'Meru'" seeks to explicate Yeats's poetry in the light of Upanishadic concepts "Shreyas," "Preyas," "Para" and "Apara". This is an example of Indian approach to W.B. Yeats.

C.T. Indra's paper, "A Woman Lost: A Reading of the Maud Gonne Poems of Yeats" seeks to explore Yeats-Maud Gonne relationship poem after poem. She rightly states that "Maud Gonne is apotheosized in several ways in Yeats's poetry". Prabhat K. Singh's "The Poetry of Unageing Intellect" discusses Yeats primarily as an Irish poet. Singh also highlights Yeats' development as a poet. Mohan Ramanan's paper lays stress on "Eastern 1916" and analyses Yeats's political option.

Prashant K. Sinha examines Yeats's plays in the light of Yeats's political beliefs. He brings a correlation between Yeats's plays and poetry on the questions of Yeats's political convictions.

Haladhar Panda explains the basic concepts of Dhvani theory and applies this theory to Yeats's poetry. He analyses a number of poems such as "The Wild Swans at Coole", "The Second Coming", "Leda and the Swan", "Lapis Lazuli" and a few others to show how Yeats's poetry can be read in the light of Dhvani theory with pleasure and profit.

Bijay Kumar Das examines the question of Yeats's moving away from personality to impersonality paving the way for reconfiguring Yeats, the man and Yeats the humanist in his poetry.

Rajnath examines the question of personality and impersonality in the poetry of Yeats and Eliot *vis-à-vis* their criticism. It is a comparative study of the two outstanding poets of the twentieth century English literature.

To conclude, I would like to say, why Yeats is relevant to the twenty-first century. That is because, Yeats has five things that are perfectly clear: precision of language, aptness of imagery, sense of tradition, love of art and longing for immortality. Apart from these, Yeats's insight into human nature, passion for full-blooded love, desire for establishing an identity both individual and national go a long way in achieving university for his poetry.

Yeats's poetry has a dream-like quality. It not only moves us but governs our mood. Reading at midnight it makes us feel like falling in love with a woman intensely and passionately but reading during the morning it prompts us to separate the art from the artist, the personal from the impersonal. What triumphs in the end is not the poet, who is bound to a woman—not here but here before, who wrote, "the world will thank me for not marrying you but go on writing me", but the poetry which transcended place and time and above all, became his 'after life'. That's the hallmark of Yeats's poetry.

2

Yeats's Response to Thoreau: Appropriations, Assimilations, Parallels and Convergences

R.W. Desai

Yeats's reading of *Walden* in "The Lake Isle of Innisfree" 1890 (Francis 12; Glick 164; Jeffares 32-34) and "The Wild Swans at Coole" 1916 (Shanley 361) has been noted, but an earlier work, his novelette *John Sherman* completed in 1888, has not received the critical attention it deserves, being merely mentioned by Shanley in passing, despite its considerable imbibing of both the thought and language of *Walden*. Further, though the two early works ("Lake Isle" and *John Sherman*) are lightweights, they are, nevertheless, stepping-stones to Yeats's later masterpieces which reflect Thoreau's continuing subtle and pervasive influence, going beyond the Irish poet's nostalgia for a pastoral life to a recognition of Thoreau particularly, among several other American authors, as pioneers breaking new ground in directions other than those taken by England and Europe. Accordingly, if I seem to spend a disproportionately long time on *John Sherman,* this is only because the work has been ignored in terms of Yeats's interest in Thoreau, and because the central thought of the work recurs—though in different manifestations—in Yeats's later works. Nearly two decades after *John Sherman* was published, his depression over Maud Gonne's rejection of his oft-repeated marriage proposal and his reading, or recollection, of a scene from the chapter "Spring" in *Walden* form the locus of one of his most exquisite and technically perfect poems, "The Wild Swans at Coole".

At this time circumstantial evidence seems to indicate that Yeats was reading Thoreau's *Journal,* written from 1841 onwards and published in 1906 in 14 volumes, in which Thoreau's disappointment over Ellen Sewall's rejection of his marriage proposal mirrors what Yeats himself was suffering. Does this link between the two suitors account for the echoes in Yeats's poem? Shortly thereafter Yeats's marriage in October 1917 to Georgie Hyde-Lees, whose mediumship was instrumental in radically changing the course of his interests by opening up a new area of esoteric knowledge and experience through her automatic writing, resulted in the publication of his metaphysical work *A Vision* in 1925. In this extraordinary book, now at the summit of his poetic achievement, Yeats quotes almost verbatim a passage from the chapter "Higher Laws" in *Walden* relating to his reading of the personality of Walt Whitman. This important reference, too, has, as far as I know, been merely noted (Shanley 364 n. 5), but not analysed. That Yeats during the period of his greatest creative energy turned to Thoreau is indicative of his close reading and assimilation of what in Thoreau reinforced and confirmed his own understanding of the composite, complex and contradictory nature of human personality.

The subject matter of this remarkable chapter, arguably the most confessional and unconventional, even shocking, of all of Thoreau's writings is, as I hope to demonstrate, refracted in some of Yeats's outstanding poems in "The Tower" section of this period, the decade of the 1920s, as well as in the equally shocking and arresting poetry of his later periods. This paper will offer what Richard Ellmann, writing in a different context, has described as "speculations, conjectures, hypotheses," going on to say that "the attempt to connect disparate elements, to describe the movements within the mind as if they were movements within the atom, to label the most elusive particles, will become more venturesome" (*Golden* 15). My venture, I dare say, will be the first serious and bold attempt to probe beneath the surface of superficial verbal borrowings of Yeats from Thoreau and uncover latent assimilations of thought and feeling that bring these two outstanding authors into a common fold.

Concerning *John Sherman*, Yeats wrote to Katharine Tynan in 1891, "If Sherman gets printed, I shall be greatly pleased. There is more of myself in it than in anything I have done" (*Letters* 165). The plot of the novel is simple, even amusing. John lives in Ireland in the village of Ballah with his mother. Fond of gardening he is, however, tempted by his rich uncle's invitation to come to London and work for him in his flourishing ship-broker's business. There John hopes "to persuade some girl with money to fall in love with me" (46). The plan works, but Margaret is a party loving girl and John is soon repelled by the glitter of London life. He now longs to return to Ballah, "take a farm and turn farmer" (106) and marry Mary, the girl he left behind in Ballah. He cleverly extricates himself from Margaret's grip by dressing shabbily, shunning London society, and introducing her to his extrovertist friend, the Reverend William Howard. Margaret loses interest in John, and he returns to Ballah and to Mary.

From this brief summary, echoes from *Walden* may be glimpsed. The seed planted in Yeats's mind by his father reading to him "some passages out of *Walden*" when he was a boy, grew into the wish "to live some day in a cottage on a little island called Innisfree" (*Autobiographies* 71-72). Like John Sherman, Yeats detested London. He wrote to Katharine Tynan with a touch of whimsy, "It is pleasant to think that this letter will go away out of this horrid London and get to the fields and rattle away in the basket.... I wish I could myself up and go in it. A ghost they say, you know, can hide in a diamond, or any such small thing" (*Collected Letters* 52). While the "nine bean-rows" of "The Lake Isle of Innisfree" are a direct reference to Thoreau's "I came to love my rows of beans" (155), Yeats's description of John Sherman's attachment to his garden has less overt but, nevertheless, latent echoes from *Walden*:

> Every morning he [John Sherman] worked in that garden among the sights and sounds of nature. Month by month he planted and hoed and dug there. (51)

In *Walden,* Thoreau tells us, his beans

> already planted, were impatient to be hoed, for the earliest had grown considerably.... I cherish them, I hoe

> them, early and late. I have an eye to them; and this is my day's work. (155)

Correspondingly, Thoreau-like, John Sherman's morning is spent in his garden "and in the afternoon [he] went out to shoot or walk.... Later on he read. He had not many books...a Shakespeare, Mungo Parks's travels, a few two-shilling novels, Percy's *Reliques,* and a volume on etiquette" (51). As we recall, Thoreau had declared that hunting "was one of the best parts of my education" (212), and in the chapter "Reading" he celebrates books among which are Homer and Shakespeare (104).

The dichotomy in *John Sherman* is the choice to be made between the "theatres, operas, parties" of London and "the country house of his dreams and of the garden" in Ballah (72-73). John Sherman's rejection of the former, like that of Thoreau's "to live deep and suck out all the marrow of life" (91), is an endorsement of *Walden's* message that seems to have remained with Yeats throughout his life. And yet, like Thoreau who after a two-year stay at the pond returned to the city, Yeats's projection of himself in the persona of John Sherman is not total; there is a part of him residing in the fashionable Reverend William Howard as well, the novel thus being more complex than might appear on the surface, a divided self that Thoreau addresses in *Walden* and that Yeats makes one of the dominant themes in his theory of the *Will* and the *Mask,* both in his *A Vision* (1925) and in his later poetry, especially as Finneran has noted, "in the two Byzantium poems" (20). *John Sherman*, however, is a preliminary work that Yeats himself in later years viewed dismissively, as he did "Innisfree" that "gave him some embarrassment later in life" (Kelly 121), and concerning *John Sherman,* entertaining "doubts about the artistic value of the book," as remarked by Finneran (12), yet, as I shall try to show in the following pages, containing in embryonic form themes that he developed and expressed in the memorable poetic style of his later compositions.

That for authors like Yeats and Thoreau, combined with their philosophy of life was an equal concern with the craft of writing is a factor not to be overlooked. Thus Yeats, early in his career, looked to the American literary scene as an exemplar for the creation of an Irish national literature. In 1892, he wrote to the editor of *United Ireland* refuting Douglas Hyde's belief that an Irish national literature written in English would be an impossibility, mentioning Whitman and Thoreau, among others, as representative of a vigorous, energetic American literature:

> America, with no past to speak of, a mere *parvenu* among the nations, is creating a national literature which in its most characteristic products differs almost as much from English literature as does the literature of France. Walt Whitman, Thoreau, Bret Harte and [George Washington] Cable, to name no more, are very American, and yet America was once an English colony (*Collected Letters* 339).

Then when Yeats visited America for the first time in 1903 on a lecture tour, he particularly noted the prevalence of "values" that owed their birth to "Thoreau and Emerson":

> Everywhere in America...one finds people who are of one's own tribe, liberated souls.... The words of Morris and of Ruskin have found hearers who have listened better because of Thoreau and Emerson; and everywhere one finds one's own table of values (America 53).

That Yeats intended his novel to be symbolic in terms of "values" is clear from his letter to Katharine Tynan of 1891:

> I am rather anxious about *Sherman*. It is good, I believe, but it will be a toss-up how the reviewers take it—for if they look for the ordinary stuff of novels they will find nothing (*Letters* 174).

On a track parallel to that of Yeats, Thoreau had noted in his *Journal* in 1856, "my work is writing, and I do not hesitate, though I know that no subject is too trivial for me" (Vol. 9, 121). Of course, it can be contended that such a commitment to the art of writing is not unique to either Thoreau or Yeats, but when the parallel tracks converge—as I hope to demonstrate later—Yeats's recognition of Thoreau's genius (along with that of Whitman and Emerson, as noted above) will become apparent. Melissa Sexton has perceptively shown that Thoreau's writing embodies the "complex relationship between the material world and language...the central constitutive role of the writer while also insisting on the full material reality of a world external to the observer" (16). This double preoccupation with writerly skill and the outside world becomes distinctively manifest in both *Walden* and *John Sherman*. For Thoreau, as for Yeats, the writer is a creator, not a mere amanuensis. Quite apart from his profession as surveyor, carpenter, or "to collect the sand by cart-loads, to make sand-paper with," Thoreau in *Walden* sees himself as a craftsman with words who, "by the perpetual instilling and drenching of the reality which surrounds us," creates a new and unfamiliar reality through language "which will explain our miracles and reveal new ones" (197, 97, 108 seriatim). The notion of the transformative power of words to metamorphose reality into a miracle is a process that the "artist in the city of Kouroo" (326) effects, shared by the "Miracle, bird or golden handiwork" of Yeats's "Byzantium" where, as I shall argue in greater detail, the tracks converge.

But prior to this stage of his poetic career in which Yeats arrived at the notion of detachment and impersonality so essential for artistic perfection, his long distress over Maud Gonne's refusal to become his wife came to a climax with her marriage to Major John MacBride. In this crisis, I see his turning to Thoreau—who had undergone a similar painful experience—as the key with which to unlock the secret of the debt that his poem "The Wild Swans at Coole" owes to *Walden's* chapter "Spring".

II

As readers of Yeats know from his poetry, prose writings, and his biographers, from 1889 onwards when he first met Maud Gonne and fell in love with her, he was emotionally tormented by her repeated rejections of his marriage proposals: "Sweetheart, do not love too long:/ I loved long and long,/ And grew to be out of fashion/ Like an old song" ("O Do Not Love Too Long") he wrote in 1905, and in 1912-14, addressing his ancestors, "Pardon that for a barren passion's sake,/ Although I have come close on forty-nine,/ I have no child, I have nothing but a book,/ Nothing but that to prove your blood and mine" ("Pardon Old Fathers"). In *Autobiographies*, he records his depression over the infructuous love affair: "I was involved in a miserable love affair, that had... absorbed my thoughts for years past.... My devotion might as well have been offered to an image in a milliner's window" (399). The poems of this early period—"When You Are Old" (1891), "A Dream of Death" (1891), or "The White Birds" (1892)—capture his anguish and frustration, whereas in "The Wild Swans at Coole" written 24 years later the poet is nostalgic but not frustrated. In 1903, Maud had unexpectedly married Major John MacBride—"a drunken, vainglorious lout" ("Easter 1916"), as Yeats understandably and eloquently described him. Yeats was devastated. Nurtured back to emotional health by the ministrations of Lady Gregory in her elegant Georgian mansion in Coole Park with its lake and surrounded by stately old trees, this was the setting for his poem "The Wild Swans at Coole" which combines both pain and ecstasy: "The trees are in their autumn beauty,/ The woodland paths are dry,/ Under the October twilight the water/ Mirrors a still sky;/ Upon the brimming water among the stones/ Are nine-and-fifty swans."

As Shanley has convincingly shown, Yeats either recollected a passage from the chapter "Spring" in *Walden,* or re-read the chapter, since the overlappings of Yeats's description of the fifty-nine swans and Thoreau's "twenty-nine" geese, along with unmistakable echoes in words, phrases, and syntax indicate that he was deeply stirred by Thoreau's vivid description of the geese that alighted on the pond (361). However, apart from noting these striking correspondences, Shanley does not ask the all important question: why, in this phase of despondency, did Yeats turn to Thoreau? The question goes to the heart of the matter, and surely informed speculation is justified in the absence of smoking-gun evidence to establish his having recollected, or having re-read, with such astonishing verbal accuracy the movements of Thoreau's twenty-nine geese that so insidiously permeate the poem.

A plausible answer might be that his longing for Maud having proved futile, he saw a kindred distress in Thoreau's failure with Ellen Sewall, the girl who on his death-bed he declared he had "always loved" (Nelson 15). As I have suggested above, perhaps Yeats was at this time reading Thoreau's *Journal* which was published in 1906 in 14 volumes. Given Yeats's continuing interest in *Walden,* this need not surprise us. Glick has pointed out that "it is rather singular that John Butler Yeats [the poet's father] should have known of *Walden* at all during his son's youth.... If his father had read *Walden* to him, therefore, the reading must have been done from a copy of the first edition, 1854, or from the first American reprinting of 1864, and neither of these editions had been large. Even in America before 1875 *Walden* had not achieved a wide distribution" (164). Accordingly, the capturing of Yeats's attention by Thoreau's recently published *Journal* containing the record of his emotional involvement with Ellen, initially reciprocated by her but later withdrawn, is likely since Yeats himself was undergoing the same agonizing experience.

Recently Nelson has told the sad story of Thoreau and Ellen Sewall.

> They'd known each other before, but they were only children then. And when the Sewall family came to Concord in July 1839, for a two-week summer vacation, things were different.... She was seventeen now, and Henry twenty-two. They spent a lot of time together in those two weeks, though they were rarely, if ever, alone. He took her for rides in his boat on the river, though Aunt Prudence went along.... The next summer, he apparently got her out in the boat alone, and he played his flute for her as they drifted on the river.

He wrote in his *Journal*: "The other day I rowed in my boat a free—even lovely young lady—and as I plied the oars she sat in the stern—and there was nothing but she between me and the sky. So might all our lives be picturesque if they were free enough" (14). Pointing out that simultaneously John, Thoreau's elder brother was also interested in Ellen, Nelson goes on to say,

> In a brotherly dynamic hard for us to understand, the younger brother deferred to the older. Ellen accepted John's proposal at first, probably because she was too surprised to turn him down, but her parents were old-line conservative Unitarians, and they wouldn't have her marrying into the Emersonian crowd. Ellen, meanwhile, decided that it wasn't John, but Henry, whom she

> preferred. This is all complex, and shadowy too; there are mysteries here that will never be explained. But after John was rejected, Henry proposed, by letter, and then, after suspense and more parental influence, he was, by letter, turned down too. Later Ellen wrote, "I never felt so badly at sending a letter in my life." But she turned him down (14).

Some of these details Nelson derives from Walter Harding's biography of Thoreau published in 1983 which, of course, Yeats never saw. But a deeply moving passage from Thoreau's *Journal* might have caught his attention. Thoreau writes:

> To sigh under the cold cold moon for a love unrequited, is to put a slight upon nature; the natural remedy would be to fall in love with the moon and the night, and find our love requited (Vol. 1, 223).

And, according to Harding, a detail which Nelson includes in his article, "when he was dying his sister mentioned Ellen's name, and he said, 'I have always loved her. I have always loved her'" (15). The parallels between the Yeats-Maud and Thoreau-Ellen situations are striking, and these along with the echoes in "The Wild Swans at Coole" from the chapter "Spring" in *Walden* would seem to explain why Yeats turned to Thoreau for consolation during the period of depression following Maud's rejection of his suit and marriage to Major John MacBride.

It only remains for us to consider briefly the poems that resulted from the futile longing that both poets experienced. Yeats's poem, "The Wild Swans at Coole," the first stanza of which I have quoted, reflects the sense of loss through the objective correlative—to use Eliot's terminology—of the swans as they "all suddenly mount/ And scatter wheeling in great broken rings/ Upon their clamorous wings" when he tries to count them; their sudden disruption and disorder being a projection of the shock he felt, while delivering a public lecture, when informed of Maud's marriage: "When, the ears being deafened, the sight of the eyes blind,/ With lightning, you went from me" ("Reconciliation"). However, "The Wild Swans at Coole" concludes on a note of serenity: "But now they drift on the still water,/ Mysterious, beautiful," reflecting the poet's acceptance of Maud's determination to find fulfillment in leading her life the way she wanted.

The subtleties of Yeats's poem are well matched by Thoreau's poem "Low in the Eastern Sky" that he included in "Sunday" of *A Week on the Concord and Merrimack Rivers.* Addressed to Ellen, unlike Yeats's poem in which the swans have multiple symbolic meanings, Thoreau's poem has throughout a note of quiet resignation, of acceptance, yet there are undercurrents that hint at the poet's awareness of Ellen having been attracted to him, but hindered by oppositional family pressures. The opening stanza's first and last four lines embody this conflict: "Low in the eastern sky/ Is set thy glancing eye;/ And though its gracious light/ Ne'er riseth to my sight,/ Yet every star that climbs/ Above the gnarled limbs/ Of yonder bill,/ Conveys thy gentle will." Whereas Yeats's poem eliminates Maud as a person, camouflaging her behind the symbolic swans, Ellen's presence pervades Thoreau's poem. A sense of loss is predominant, but the poet is not despondent, for, as the penultimate stanza affirms, "Still will I strive to be/ As if thou wert with me;/ Whatever path I take,/ It shall be for thy sake,/ Of gentle slope and wide,/ As thou wert by my side,/ Without a root/ To trip thy gentle foot" (36). Both poems are memorable, each in its own distinctive way.

But a further question remains to be addressed. What might have been the link between Yeats's 59 swans and Thoreau's 29 geese, the two numbers having the common numeral 9? Given Yeats's interest in numerology, to which his *A Vision* bears ample testimony, surely the question demands an answer, necessarily speculative. Two possibilities come to mind: (1) the "nine bean-rows" of "The Lake Isle of Innisfree" are obviously derived from the chapter "The Bean-Field" of *Walden,* but more to the point, Thoreau locates his supreme chapter "The Ponds" at the very heart of the book as chapter 9 which is at the centre of its 18 chapters, and he invests the pond and its surroundings with a mystical aura: "When I was four years old, as I well remember, I was brought from Boston...through these very woods and this field, to the pond. It is one of the oldest scenes stamped on my memory...and even I have at length helped to clothe that fabulous landscape of my infant dreams" (155-56). As a poet of memory and imagination Yeats could well have responded to Thoreau's immortalization of Walden Pond through his marvellous deployment of language. Four months before his death, in "Under Ben Bulben" (September 1938), Yeats too celebrated the transformative power of language in words that endorse Thoreau's claim: "Where everything that meets the eye,/ Flowers and grass and cloudless sky,/ Resemble forms that are or seem/ When sleepers wake and yet still dream,/ And when it's vanished still declare,/ With only bed and bedstead there,/ The heavens had opened" (2). *Walden* was published in 1854; exactly 59 years later in 1913 Yeats wrote "September 1913" in which "the wild geese" of stanza 3 refer to the Irish emigrants setting out for America, but it was never beyond Yeats to compress more than one meaning into a symbol, and the 59 swans of "The Wild Swans at Coole" could well be a private salute to the spirit of the dead Thoreau. In a letter to Katharine Tynan on the subject of symbolism, he wrote, "Under disguise of symbolism I have said several things to which only I have the key" (Tynan 47). Two years after "September 1913" he was writing "The Wild Swans at Coole" in which the 59 swans are an echo of Thoreau's 29 geese. Yeats frequently affirmed the continuing presence of the spirits of the dead among the living: "Our shadows rove the gravel still,/ The living seem more shadowy than they" ("The New Faces"), and in "All Souls' Night," "A ghost may come;/ For it is a ghost's right,/ His element is so fine...." In his capacity as a Senator in Ireland's Parliament, during a debate on divorce when he mentioned the case of Parnell having married a divorcee in justification for the repealing of the country's outdated and restrictive law, a fellow senator objected: "Do you not think we might leave the dead alone?" Yeats's reply was swift and categoric: "I am passing on. I would hate to leave the dead alone" (*Senate Speeches* 98).

III

Emerging from his earlier period of depression over his failure with Maud Gonne, Yeats now embarked upon a new poetic and intellectual adventure with an imaginative energy that he poured into the poems written from this time onwards, as well as into the writing of the complex *A Vision* (1925) with its subjective judgement of prominent human personalities, assigning them to their appropriate phases from 1 to 28. However, at certain phases, 1 to 5 and 15 and 28, "there's no human life," the ghostly instructors pointed out, the examples given for these phases being of mythological figures like "great Brama," or of characters in literature like "Don Juan" or "the fool of Shakespeare" (40, 46, 115-16 seriatim). But from phase 6 onwards "actual men and women" (xii) begin to feature as examples, Whitman being the first who he assigns to this phase. In his analysis of Whitman's personality, Yeats juxtaposes the following passage from the chapter "Higher Laws" in *Walden*:

> The other day I picked up the lower jaw of a hog, with white and sound teeth and tusks, which suggested that there was an animal health and vigor distinct from the spiritual. (219)

In *A Vision* (1925), quoting Thoreau almost verbatim, Yeats writes:

> Had Walt Whitman lived out of phase, desire to prove that all his emotions were healthy and intelligible, to set his practical sanity above all not made in his fashion, to cry "thirty years old and in perfect health!" would have turned him into some kind of jibing demagogue; and to think of him would be to remember that Thoreau when he had picked up the jaw-bone of a pig that had not a tooth missing, recorded that there also was perfect health (46-47 [also quoted in *A Vision,* 1937, with a minor change: instead of "not a tooth missing", "no tooth missing" 113]).

In order to clarify his reason for not seeing Whitman as a health freak with a single track mind, but rather, as a complex personality, Yeats refers to the chapter "Higher Laws" in *Walden* which contains Thoreau's most candid and self-revelatory statement in all of his writings, portraying himself as a combination of opposites, a description that suited Yeats's current thought. Thoreau writes:

> As I came through the woods with my string of fish.... I caught a glimpse of a woodchuck stealing across my path, and felt a strange thrill of savage delight, and was strongly tempted to seize and devour him raw; not that I was hungry then.... I found in myself, and still find, an instinct toward a higher, or, as it is named, spiritual life, as do most men, and another toward a primitive rank and savage one, and I reverence them both (210).

This chapter, especially the shocking savagery of the confession by Thoreau, seems to have lodged deeply in Yeats's creative consciousness since in several of his later outstanding poems its influence may be detected, as earlier noted in *John Sherman* as well, where the idea of a divided consciousness had featured prominently. Concurrent with *A Vision* during the decade of the 1920s, the Byzantium poems appeared, including such brilliant ones as "Leda and the Swan" (1924), and "Among School Children" (1926). Even more indelibly impinging on Yeats's thought than did Thoreau's 29 geese at Walden Pond, his chapter "Higher Laws," I suggest, was influential in corroborating as well as shaping the content of the poems mentioned above. The dichotomy of personality so forcefully articulated in this pivotal chapter is both startling and the kind of frank confession that Yeats's mind would seize and relish, as becomes increasingly evident in the "Crazy Jane" and "Last Poems" sections of his *Collected Poems.*

Consider from "Higher Laws" in *Walden* these statements for their thematic commonality with Yeats's poems of the 1920s: Thoreau's "we are such gods or demigods only as fauns and satyrs, the divine allied to beasts" (220) and Yeats's "A sudden blow: the great wings beating still/ Above the staggering girl, her thighs caressed/ By the dark webs" ("Leda and the Swan"); Thoreau's "Yet the spirit can for the time pervade and control every member and function of the body, and transmute what in form is the grossest sensuality into purity and devotion" (219) and Yeats's "Labour is blossoming or dancing where/ The body is not bruised to pleasure soul, ...O body swayed to music, O brightening glance,/ How can we know the dancer from the dance?" ("Among School Children"); Thoreau's "We are so degraded that we cannot speak simply of the necessary functions of human nature. In earlier ages, in some countries, every function was reverently spoken of (221) and Yeats's "But Love has pitched his mansion in/ The place of excrement;/ For nothing can be sole or whole/ That has not been rent" ("Crazy Jane Talks with the Bishop") and "From pleasure of the bed,/ Dull as a worm,/ His rod and its butting head/ Limp as a worm" ("The Chambermaid's Second Song"); Thoreau's "We are conscious of an animal in us, which awakens in proportion as our higher nature slumbers. It is reptile and sensual" (219) and Yeats's "That I may hear if we should kiss/ A contrapuntal serpent hiss" ("The Lady's Third Song").

Focusing on "Sailing to Byzantium," we recall that the poem's arresting opening lines are a repudiation of the world that belongs to youth: "That is no country for old men. The young/ In one another's arms." Extravagant, even bizarre, the poem generates an extraordinary, defiant assertiveness that drives the poet's ship to sail the seas "and come/ To the holy city of Byzantium," a city of the mind, of "unageing intellect," like the poet's ancient Norman tower in Thoor Ballylee that he purchased for thirty-five pounds in 1916 and, in a letter to Sturge Moore, regarded as a powerful symbol of his own advancing age as well "as a permanent symbol of my work plainly visible to the passer-by. As you [Sturge Moore who was designing the cover for the poems in *The Tower*] know all my art theories depend upon just this rooting of mythology in the earth" (Ellmann, *Identity* 147). Twenty years later he re-affirmed this belief in "The Municipal Gallery Revisited" with the lines "John Synge, I and Augusta Gregory, thought/ All that we did, all that we said or sang/ Must come from contact with the soil, from that/ Contact everything Antaeus-like grew strong," echoing Thoreau's love for his beans: "They attached me to the earth, and so I got strength like Antaeus" (155).

"Sailing to Byzantium," though addressing a different pair of contrasts—youth and age—from those in *John Sherman*-materialistic success and the contemplative life—have one factor in common, a choice to be made, which is also the essence of

Walden. The solipsism of "studying/ Monuments of its own magnificence" signifies a turning inwards upon itself by the soul, and surely this is one of the main themes of *Walden* as defined in the book's most ethereal and mystical chapter "The Ponds" where Thoreau declares, "I am its stony shore" and, addressing his own reflection in the water, "can almost say, Walden, is it you?" (193). These key lines in which author and pond merge and become one, give birth, so to speak, to the book *Walden* that Thoreau regards as the repository of his enduring identity for posterity, a metamorphosis he states unambiguously toward the book's end:

> I do not suppose that I have attained to obscurity, but I should be proud if no more fatal fault were found with my pages on this score than was found with the Walden ice (325).

And in "Higher Laws" he asserts what might seem an uncomfortable truth, that the greatest works of art owe their origin to the carnal elements embedded in the human psyche. "We are all sculptors and painters," he tells us, "and our material is our own flesh and blood and bones" (221). Does not Yeats make the same admission a year before his death in the closing lines of "The Circus Animals' Desertion": "Now that my ladder's gone,/ I must lie down where all the ladders start,/ In the foul rag-and-bone shop of the heart"?

The metempsychosis of Thoreau the man into *Walden* the book may well be seen as the predecessor of Yeats's projection of himself after death as being gathered "into the artifice of eternity" in the form of a prophetic bird made by "Grecian goldsmiths" "of hammered gold and gold enamelling...to sing/ Of what is past, or passing, or to come." If Yeats chooses to travel to Byzantium/Constantinople for such a timeless transformation, Thoreau had earlier chosen to travel yet farther east to India, the land of "the sacred water of the Ganges" (298), identifying himself with the artist in the city of Kouroo who, in his search for the perfect stick is endowed, "without his knowledge, with perennial youth". When he had finished "his work, it suddenly expanded before the gaze of the astonished artist into the fairest of all the creations of Brahma". The notion of art as timeless finds an unmistakable correspondence of expression and thought in both Thoreau and Yeats. The "stick" that the artist in the city of Kouroo takes centuries to bring to perfection till it is transformed into a "staff is—similar to Yeats's prophetic bird—adorned with precious stones.... The material was pure; how could the result be other than wonderful?," Thoreau asks (326-27).

As Daniel S. Malachuk has persuasively argued, Thoreau the Transcendentalist is opposed to relativist and contingent notions of progress by society, and upholds the individual's prerogative in making the choice for right conduct, behaviour, and action as indicated by *Nature* (288-89). Thus, the artist of Kouroo is no dreamer. "He had made a new System in making a staff, a world with full and fair proportions; in which, though the old cities and dynasties had passed away, fairer and more glorious ones had taken their places" (327). The same may be said of Yeats's Byzantium poems. Far from being escapist, the protagonist of "Sailing to Byzantium" will sing "Of what is past, or passing, or to come." As a keen observer of two vast historical cycles covering a span of nearly 4000 years, the first commencing with the rape of Leda by Zeus the Swan, the second the impregnation of Mary by the Dove ("The Mother of God"), Yeats has an uncanny insight into the forces shaping history. Only six years earlier he had written "The Second Coming," an apocalyptic and terrifying vision of the "rough beast" emerging from the political violence in Ireland and Russia, culminating in the Easter Uprising of 1916, followed by the Russian revolution of 1917 during which more than 500 members of the bourgeoisie were shot in Petrograd as a reprisal for the attack on Lenin.

A similar transformation of the "stick" into a "staff" by Thoreau's artist is effected in Yeats's later poem "Byzantium": the bird "of hammered gold and gold enamelling" of the earlier poem will now "scorn aloud/ In glory of changeless metal/ Common bird or petal/ And all complexities of mire or blood." Thus was effected "the transmutation of life into art," Yeats had written many years earlier in a different but thematically related context, "and a cry of measureless desire for a world made wholly of essences" (*Mythologies* 267). For both Yeats and Thoreau the finished product, the artifacts that both writers leave behind for posterity, are their permanent legacies in a world of time and change.

"I am thankful," Thoreau writes, "that this pond was made deep and pure for a symbol" (287), and so significant are the pond's dimensions in terms of its essence as noted by the surveyor (Thoreau's profession) that "the two diameters draw lines through the length and breadth of the aggregate of a man's particular daily behaviors and waves of life into his coves and inlets, and where they intersect will be the height or depth of his character" (291). Thus does Thoreau's pond mutate into *Walden* the book, becoming the touchstone whereby each reader may measure his/her "height or depth" of character, comparable to the manner in which Yeats's symbolic book *A Vision* (1925), a map of human character and personality, mutated into the remarkable poems of the 1920s decade, thus embodying the essence of the book. Yeats's ghostly instructors, as he himself tells us, warned him not to spend the rest of his life "explaining and piecing together" their messages, which he had offered to do: "'No', was the answer, 'we have come to give you metaphors for poetry'" (*A Vision* 1937: 8). For both Thoreau and Yeats, the final product, the work of art, are the book *Walden,* and the poems of the 1920s, respectively: they are the essences that will defy time.

In passing, it needs to be pointed out that the quest for perfection may be seen not only in Thoreau's craftsmanship as writer, but even in the more mundane activity of a pencil manufacturer as a young man. Emerson, in his obituary for Thoreau, recalled that since Thoreau's father was a manufacturer of lead pencils, Thoreau, just out of college, had joined the factory:

> believing he could make a better pencil than was then in use. After completing his experiments, he exhibited his work to chemists and artists in Boston, and having obtained their certificates to its excellence and to its equality with the best London manufacture, he returned home contented. His friends congratulated him that he had now opened his way to fortune. But he replied, that he should never make another pencil. "Why should I? I

> would not do again what I have done once." He resumed his endless walks and miscellaneous studies.... (266)

Like the artist in the city of Kouroo, he had attained his goal.

IV

Influence study is subjective and therefore hazardous. Writers seldom acknowledge their debts to their creditors. Bloom has gone to the extent of naming this guilt consciousness as "anxiety" (9-10). Often, despite attempts by authors to conceal, disguise, or even deny that they are susceptible, the truth can be sensed and may, in fact, be more of an absorption, an assimilation, than direct influence. Thus, if we ask why Yeats, while writing *A Vision,* went back to his recollection of Thoreau's chapter "Higher Laws," mentioning Thoreau by name, and quoting a passage from it, or, yet more likely, had been re-reading *Walden,* the answer might be, because he found in Thoreau's bold declaration that he saw in himself both the "spiritual" and the "savage," "and I revered them both" (210), a truth that Yeats himself had arrived at through introspection and which constitutes the strength of his later poetry. Further, Thoreau's outspokenness gave impetus to his own theory of the *Will* and the *Mask,* the confrontation between opposites tentatively adumbrated in *John Sherman,* and much later triumphantly asserted in "Sailing to Byzantium" where the choice for the vigorous intellect of old age in preference to the sensuality of youth is declared in a tone of defiance of nature's gerontric compulsion. To Yeats the structure of *Walden* would have exerted an immense appeal, the configuration of its chapters in oppositional juxtaposition to each other: "Solitude" followed by "Visitors," "The Ponds" followed by "Baker Farm," "Higher Laws" followed by "Brute Neighbors," Thoreau thus recording, and celebrating the same keen awareness of the duality and inner struggle of human personality. Thus, Yeats's early engagement with Thoreau in the writing of *John Sherman* was not just a passing phase, but had a broad base: the essence of this engagement re-surfaced in the long journey of his intellectual development, the evidence of its latent presence being circumstantial: a convergence of thought rather than a mirroring.

If it is right to describe "Higher Laws" as the most confessional writing of Thoreau's, then Yeats's four-line poem "The Spur" (1936) is equally confessional. Addressed to critics of his sexuality on account of the operation he underwent which, "it was claimed, could restore the sexual emerges of the elderly" (Aldritt 329), he wrote, "You think it horrible that lust and rage/ Should dance attendance upon my old age;/ They were not such a plague when I was young:/ What else have I to spur me into song?" Understandably, T.S. Eliot was not amused by Yeats's cheeky wit and irony, yet had the candour to admit, "To what honest man, old enough, can these sentiments be entirely alien? They can be subdued and disciplined by religion, but who can say that they are dead?" (302). But for both Yeats and Thoreau "religion" would be Nature, though Eliot would certainly disagree.

The convergences between Yeats and Thoreau's thought are too close to be dismissed as coincidental. Concerning the Irish poet Brian Merriman's lines on bastardy in one of his poems, Yeats observed that "the bastard's speech in *Lear* is floating through his mind" (*Explorations* 285). With equal assurance can it be said of some of Yeats's best work that the spirit of *Walden* is floating through his mind.

Works Cited

Alldritt, Keith. *W.B. Yeats: The Man and the Milieu.* London: John Murray, 1977. Print.

Bloom, Harold. *A Map of Misreading.* New York: Oxford University Press, 1975. Print.

Eliot, T.S. "The Poetry of W.B. Yeats." 1940. Rpt. *The Permanence of Yeats.* Ed. James Hall and Martin Steinmann. New York: Collier Books, 1961. Print.

Ellmann, Richard. *Golden Codgers: Biographical Speculations.* London: Oxford University Press, 1973. Print.

——. *The Identity of Yeats.* New York: Oxford University Press, 1964. Print.

Emerson, Ralph Waldo. "Thoreau." *Walden and Civil Disobedience.* Ed. Owen Thomas. New Delhi: Prentice-Hall of India, 1986. Print.

Finneran, Richard J. Ed. *John Sherman and Dhoya.* By W.B. Yeats. Detroit: Wayne State University Press, 1969. Print.

Francis, Robert. "Of *Walden* and Innisfree." *Christian Science Monitor* (November 6, 1952), 12-13. Print.

Click, Wendell. "Yeats's Early Reading of *Walden.*" *Boston Public Library Quarterly,* 5 (July 1953): 164-66. Print.

Jeffares, A. Norman. *A Commentary on the Collected Poems of W.B. Yeats.* Stanford: Stanford University Press, 1968. Print.

Kelly, John. Ed. *The Collected Letters of W.B. Yeats: 1865-1895.* Vol. 1. Oxford: Clarendon Press, 1986. Print.

Malachuk, Daniel S. "Transcendentalism, Perfectionism, and *Walden.*" *The Concord Saunterer.* Vols. 12/13 (2004/2005): 283-303. Print.

Nelson, Howard. "Stories." *Thoreau Society Bulletin.* No. 282 (Summer 2013): 14-15. Print.

Sexton, Melissa. "'Making the Earth Say Beans': Thoreau's 'The Bean-Field' as Latourian Mobilization." *Thoreau Society Bulletin.* No. 285 (Spring 2014): 16. Print.

Shanley, J. Lyndon. "Thoreau's Geese and Yeats's Swans." *American Literature,* 30:3 (November 1958): 361-64. Print.

Thoreau, Henry D. *The Illustrated Walden with Photographs from the Gleason Collection.* Ed. J. Lyndon Shanley. Princeton University Press, 1973. Print.

——. *The Journal of Henry David Thoreau.* 14 vols. Ed. Bradford Torrey and Francis H. Allen. Boston: Houghton Mifflin, 1906. Print.

——. *A Week on the Concord and Merrimack Rivers.* Ed. Walter Harding. New York: Holt, Rinehart and Winston, 1963. Print.

Tynan, Katharine. *The Middle Years.* London: Constable, 1916. Print.

Yeats, W.B. "America and the Arts." *Metropolitan Magazine,* XXII (April 1905): 53-60. Print.

——. *Autobiographies.* London: Macmillan, 1955. Print.

——. *The Collected Letters of W.B. Yeats: 1865-1895.* Vol. I. Ed. John Kelly and Eric Domville. Oxford: Clarendon Press, 1986. Print.

——. *The Collected Poems of W.B. Yeats.* London: Macmillan, 1958. Print.

——. *A Critical Edition of Yeats's A Vision (1925).* Ed. George Mills Harper and Walter K. Hood. Rpt. London: Macmillan, 1978. Print.

——. *Explorations.* New York: Macmillan, 1962. Print.

——. *John Sherman and Dhoya.* Ed. Richard J. Finneran. Detroit: Wayne State University Press, 1969. Print.

——. *The Letters of W.B. Yeats.* Ed. Allan Wade. London: Rupert Hart-Davis, 1954. Print.

——. *Mythologies.* New York: Macmillan, 1959. Print.

——. *The Senate Speeches of W.B. Yeats.* Ed. Donald R. Pearce. Bloomington: Indiana University Press, 1960. Print.

——. *A Vision.* 1937. Rpt. London: Macmillan, 1961. Print.

3

Yeats, the Poet's Quarrel with Himself

S. Viswanathan

It would seem to facilitate our understanding and enjoyment of Yeats's work to view it in the perspective of the antinomies which mark his poetry and prose essays. Roughly, these antitheses are those between such pairs as his Irishness and Europeanness, on the one hand and, on the other, Irishness/Europeanness and cosmopolitanism of international reach; personality and impersonality; romantic and modern/modernist; self or body on the one side and the soul on the other; his private mythologizing and tradition as well as the individual in him and tradition. It was Yeats who made the memorable statement: "We make out of quarrel with others, rhetoric, but of our quarrel with ourselves poetry" (Anima Hominis). It may therefore be not inept to try to view how these antinomies function in Yeats, within the compass of a short paper.

Yeats was a true-born Irishman. At the same time, his Irishness did not insulate him from a European identity and experience, and these, Irishness and Europeanness were held in imaginatively fruitful tension in his thought and feeling with several cosmopolitan-like exposures to several other cultures, especially the Hindu-Indian and Japanese traditions and aspects of their ways of life. A similar tension between Irish and Greek, the fountainhead of European culture, operated in Yeats. In one of his very last poems "The Statue", he acclaims the sense of proportion that marks Greek art and sculpture as against the formlessness, as he calls it, of Persian or Oriental art: what is interesting is that he declares in the note with which he prefixes the poem, that the Irish deity Cuchulain will come back to preserve as sense of proportion in art, in a telescoping of the roots of Irish tradition with Greek-European. It was not for nothing that he was in his younger and formative phase an avid reader of the theosophist's bible, Madam Blavatsky's *The Secret Doctrine* and *Isis Unveiled.* The elaborate private mythology and system that he built at the early stage of his great creative phase from the second decade of the twentieth century is a product of the assimilation of such a wide and deep absorption of elements of various cultural strains held in ultimate imaginative collaboration, though they may initially sound like "strains of discord". The interaction of these experiences results in a synthesis or rapprochement of these. If he in the latter half of his younger phase responded to the French *symbolistes* or the aesthetic movement in England, his innate zest for life and commitment to living ensured that these *fin-de-siecle* influences did not seep into him. He certainly would never say "As for living, let our servants do it for us". He had a basic commitment to the Irish cause and was friend and admirer of some key leaders of the Irish political movement. Yet he tended to regard the movement and its goings on, the violence and bloodshed it caused, with regret and reservation, a mark of his essential "reverence for life", which held in check his partisan sympathizes. All there apparently heterogeneous influences we may say, helped him to the acquisition of additional personalities which went into the making of the great poetic personality he was.

Once he came to feel that "the ceremony of innocence is drowned", perhaps in the floodtide of violence by way of the First World War, the Irish rebellion and the Russian Revolution, he inclined towards the ceremony of experience, vicariously though, he found in such Asian traditions as the *samurai* of Japan and its way of life with their tea ceremony and all that, and some aspects of Indian thought and modes of living such as those mediated to him through his earlier acquaintance with Mohini Chatterjee, "the Brahmin" and later more deeply, with Sri Purohit Swami, "The Indian Monk". Yeats collaborated with

Purohit Swami in his English translation of twelve *Upanishads*, by "Englishing" the translation for his friend. In several of his very early poems, Yeats handles Indian myth and legend. But in those of his maturity he makes romarkable use of the implication of Hindu symbology, especially that of the swan. The signal instance is that of "Leda and the Swan".

It is in his post-"Easter 1916" poems that Yeats comes to explore the significances of the swan image in Indian symbology such as the bird symbolizing the soul, its immutability, eternity, immortality and perfection. In his early poems, he handles the image in conventional emblematic ways, also at the same time its connotations in Celtie myth and earlier English poetry such as Spenser's. But in the poems in his mature phase of "symbolical transformation" he draws interestingly and in complex fashion, on the symbological connotations of the swan in the Hindu tradition. He did not make anything like a systematic study of Hindu scriptures. But he got to know the essential significances of the swan idea through his conversation and a sort of collaboration with Sri Purohit Swami (*Essays and Introductions* 430 and 460). He also came across the swan as idea in Upanishads such as the Brahadaranya and the Katha, though perhaps not the idea as it occurs in *The Mahabharata*, "Moksha dharma". It is to be noted that Yeats employs the swan idea in poems such as "The Wild Swans at Coole", "Coole Park and Ballylee", "Nineteen Hundred and Nineteen", and "Leda and the Swan" besides obliquely touching upon it in the Byzantium poems. It is, however, important to remember that Yeats has perhaps also in mind the suggestions of the image in Celtic myth and the Neoplanic philosophy, which probability has been well-documented by scholars. But the operative force of the idea, suggested in Hindu tradition, is absorbed and grafted to the other sources in his poetry.

Now for a brief look at "Leda and Swan" from the point of view of the theme of this essay. In the reference earlier cited (*Essays and Introductions*), Yeats tells how Purohit Swami gave him an account of the God Dattatreya, the ideal prototype of the Yogi in Hindu tradition, manifested himself to him as Swami climbed a steep hill and started worshipping in the hill the shrine of the God at the top. The God himself ordained Swami as a *sannyasin* in the Datta order and named him, significantly, *hamsa,* the swan of Lake Manasarovar, near Mount Kailash of Siva and the Eternal Soul, at once. Purohit Swami narrates the event in great and ecstatic detail in his autobiography which was brought to light, edited and published by the late Professor Vinod Sena of Delhi University towards the end of the last century. Indeed in the chant *soham hamsah* mentioned to Yeats by Swami there is double or multiple signification. Swami rendered it as meaning—"I am the Eternal Soul, the swan". It would also amount to "I am He, He is I", a felt declaration of the Advantic faith that the individual soul and the Brahman, the Eternal soul, *jivatma* and *paramatma* are one, the non-duality. "Leda and the Swan" is a telling illustration of Yeats's fascination with the swan idea and a whole set of antinomies that marked his personality and poetry.

Leda and the Swan

A sudden blow: the great wings beating still
Above the staggering girl, her thighs caressed
By the dark webs, her nape caught in his bill.
He holds her helpless breast upon his breast.

How can those terrified vague fingers push
The leathered glory from her loosening thighs?
And how can body, laid in that white rush.
But feel the strange heart beating where it lies?

A shudder in the loins engenders there
The broken wall, the burning roof and tower
And Agamemnon dead.

Being so caught up.
So mastered by the brute blood of the air.
Did she put on his knowledge with his power
Before the indifferent beak could let her drop?
(Webb 149)

Such interesting aspects of the poem as the vivid enactment, the surprises due to the interesting combination of words and of ideas, and the syntactic and rhythmic energy, the visual inspiration behind the poem and Yeats's personal reading of the Leda myth have all been amply discussed by critics. It will do here to point out how the swan image (Jupiter or Jove as swan) in the poem holds together in suspension, and a sort of reconciliation though not resolution contraries like divinity and humanity, animality; the moment and eternity; history and eternity; knowledge and power and "brute blood" and purity.

Incidentally, now that we are on Jove as Swan, it may not be altogether irrelevant to note a connection to "Juno's swans". Shakespeare makes Celia in *As You Like It* (1.3.78) speak of "Juno's Swans", a phrase which has beaten successive editors, except Johnson who rather vaguely referred to an "old tradition" that Juno's chariot was drawn by a pair of swans. Generally, doves are supposed to draw Juno's chariot. But in Richard Lynche's *The Fountain of Fiction* (1596), which is an English rendering of an Italian dictionary of the iconology and iconography of classical gods and goddesses, it is pointed out that not only doves are thought of as drawing Juno's chariot, but some other birds such as the swan. Shakespeare must have got the idea from some such source. Lynhe's book seems to have been well enough circulated in its day. Juno must have got used to the escapes and catamorphoses of the great god husband.

Now back to our consideration of "Leda and the Swan". The contraries which Yeats grapples with and which charged the intense energy and complex effect of his poems, can perhaps, for clarity be rephrased thus, at some risk of overwriting. What Yeats faces out is the conflict between the rival claims of the eternal and the temporal, the spiritual and the physical, the way of Negation and the Way of Affirmation. It is in short "the fierce dispute between *salvation* and impassioned clay". No wonder that he should try after taking over of the eternal as well as that of an involved contact with the world, physical reality, and the flesh, attached to the swan in Indian lore. He invests it with additional significance and gives the image an additional individual meaning, exploiting the love as swan idea. He suggests that the bird signified not merely the spiritual and the eternal but a combination of the highest in the spiritual, the eternal or the divine and the floor. The image is more than that of "an artifice of eternity": it is something that participates at once in the here and now, with commitment, and in the divine and the transcendental. It thus becomes a hypostasis, a projection of an ideal hankered after by Yeats. The swan image, especially Jove as swan in his forcing himself on Leda carries the oblique suggestion of a "reconciliation of opposites". The Sanskrit word 'hamsa' for 'swan' is synonymous with 'sannyasin' or 'renunciate'. In the Indian way of life, the 'sannyasin', or for that matter the Islamic Sufi does not generally sever all contact with the world but with non-attachment yet with concern he serves as friend, philosopher and guide to the lay citizens in their secular as well as spiritual life. There are a few exceptions to this rule, however, amount the contraries with rival claims on him what assailed him most is perhaps the polarity of soul and self or body. One would not forget the monkey-gland surgery he went in for on the onset of old age, seeking rejuvenation. The conflict is well expressed in the poem "A Dialogue between the Soul and the Self". Yeats had too much of a zest for living and for the experience of the world to cultivate a contempt of the flesh and the world. The poems forcefully accept this fact. Not for him the idea of renunciation.

The interest of Yeats' poetry is in good part the interest of his personality, a great and individual personality, complex and composite in its constitution, almost multiple. Eliot, fellow leader with Yeats in modernist verse, in his memorial lecture on Yeats came to radically revise his impersonal theory of poetry enunciated in his "Tradition and the Individual Talent" some three decades before his Yeats lecture. On the basis of his mature experience of the poetry of Yeats (and of Shakespeare), he admitted that the great poetry of such as Yeats and Shakespeare includes, as it may surpass, personality and that it is only the lyrics of minor poets which can be completely impersonal. Yeats is there in every poem he wrote. Looked at another way the poems perhaps are meant to offer a release for the tensions within him, and he found some way of reconciling them in the articulation in imaginative terms of these tensions. At the same time, the creative process of the poems in their way of proceeding has ample impersonal qualities in that the words images, the ideation, rhythm, tone and syntactical movement develop in telling combination and interaction in "exploratory creative" fashion. So much so that one feels that the medium writes itself.

It is, again, a curious relationship that is to be traced between the individual, even idiosyncratic cast and orientation of his poetry and thought, and the multiplicity of traditions that he was in touch with from one phase of his career to another. There are the roots he had in Irish culture, folklore and beliefs. He was influenced deeply by the English poetic tradition especially Shakespeare and Blake. His magpie gathering of ideas and impressions from theosophical studies such as those of its founder Madam Blavatsky, *Iris Unveilds* (1870) in particular, the Kabbalsh and other arcane sources, his interest in magic experiences in the late nineteenth century practices such sconces and such other natural activities as automatic writing were part of his life. His wife acted as medium to take down automatic writing that was dictated to her by mysterious sources. With the shake-up of one's faith in the "casual creeds" of religion and European culture and civilization, he resorted to tapping such a variety of sources. He went on to build a system of his own in an effort to make sense or pattern out of human history and time and its vicissitudes using ideas such as that of the Great Memory (something like Jung's "collective unconscious") from Irish folk beliefs, the Greek cyclical view of history, and the Hindu and partly Islamic reading of the phases of the moon in their relevance for human life and observances. Yeats constituted for himself a private mythology, a system of his own. In his private life and thought he attached importance to his system. For instance, his system views time and its movement in the image of a gyre widening itself as it moves. He bought an old medieval tower in an isolated spot in Galway with a winding staircase (a gyre) on top of which he had a room with a view here he chose to stay from time to time. It is a less known tourist curiosity now. Yet the system served only as a catalytic agent in his poems, except for a few points like "The Phases of the Moon" and "Ego Dominus Tuus". For the rest, especially in his best poetry, the system at best supplied him with some images which he put to telling use, and nothing more. The poems can be read and enjoyed without reference to the system.

We may bring this brief consideration of the antinomies in Yeats a short look at that of Romantic and modernist. Yeats can with justification be called a "last Romantic". But he was surely a first and foremost modern in his post-1916 poems. It is not as though the Romantic qualities of Yeats were left behind by him in his modernist phase. The two tendencies coexist in the post-1916 poems. Certainly, he did not develop the anti-Romantic attitude which marked his fellow leader Eliot of the modernist movement. As we tried to see, Yeats could not but bring the stamp of his fascinating personality to his poetry. He did not entertain the prejudices and imperfect sympathies of Eliot and a few others with regard to Shelley. He admired the symbolism of Shelley, and it inspired him. Yeats would not have cared for the strong anti-Romantic views propounded by the New Humanist philosophers of Harvard University such as Irving Babbitt, which views in good measure shaped the young Eliot at Harvard when he was studying for his doctorate in Philosophy there. Further, Yeats was far from setting himself against the idea of seeking escape from the harshness of the contemporary world in and through poetry, though he would be the last person to take recourse to mere escapism. The anti-Romantics generally seem to have failed to realise the crucial distinction between escape and escapism. Escape is legitimate whereas escapism is negative.

The modernist tone and tenor that signally marks Yeats's post-1916 verse is unmistakable. The turns and twists, and the surprises of diction, rhythm and syntactical movement, and, above all, the precision in his verse, as noted earlier in this paper, and remarkable, and make him out to be the greatest master in modernist verse. Yet the ace modernist in Yeats is, at the same time, authentically Romantic in attitude and approach and themes. The sheer power of his poetry could fuse Romantic and modern. He is the leading example of the continuity of modern/modernist with Romantic, which continuity, as it increasingly comes to be recognized, was there alongside or despite the break with Victorian and Romantic.

Blake, a kindered spirit of Yeats, in his visionary apprehension, set great store by the dialectical play, as he saw it, of contraries in life and the human mind. Yeats viewed the interaction as dialogic.

These are examples where the antitheses seem to evaporate in the white heat of the poetic and imaginative make up of the poet as he faces them squarely.

Works Cited

Webb, Timothy, ed. *W.B. Yeats: Selected Poems*. London: Penguin Books, 1991. Print.

Yeats. "The Indian Monk" and "The Holy Mountain", *Essays and Introduction*. London: Macmillan, 1951. Print.

4

Yeats's Journey from 'Byzantium' to 'Meru'

S. Ramaswamy

> Lead me from the unreal to the real!
> Lead me from darkness to light!
> Lead me from death to immortality! (Swami and Yeats 119).
>
> Yeats's translation of the "Shanti Mantra"

I

I will begin with a personal statement. Fifty years ago (1965) when I was at the University of California in Los Angeles, I was a participant in the Yeats's Centenary Celebration conducted by my teacher, Professor Walter Starkie, a member of the Royal Society and a personal friend and mentor of W.B. Yeats. Professor Starkie, a fellow Irishman knew Yeats very well indeed and was an eye-witness of the Easter 1916 spring described by Yeats in his famous poem "Easter 1916"—it was indeed a very memorable experience.

My second experience was equally memorable. I knew through correspondence, Dr. Kathreen Reine, the great Yeats scholar, the author of *Yeats the Initiate*, a monumental work written from the point of view of the esoteric and occult in Yeats when she makes a special reference to Yeats's *Vision* and his Cosmology. In a letter to me on 23 July 1991, she said:

> I particularly appreciated your *Hamlet* paper—I have long been saying that Indian scholars have much to contribute to criticism of Western Texts, but not by the adoption of Western ideas which produce only abridged carbon-copy versions of Western Criticism, which are destructive to Indian thought and of no use whatsoever to Western Thought, although of course the universities have an industry in such things. Its all part of the intellectual imperialism of the West and one can only deplore it. (Personal Letter to the present author on 23 July 1991)

Then I take my cue from this statement and comment on Yeats's intellectual and spiritual voyage of self-discovery. Yeats was always interested in India like his friend George Russell (A.E.) who was all a part of the Irish Movement along with Lady Gregory. He says:

> For some forty years my friend George Russell (A.E.) has quoted me passages from some Upanishad, and for these forty years I have said to myself—someday I will find out if he knows what he is talking about. (*The Ten Principal Upanishads* 7)

To quote Yeats's own statement:

> When I met Shree Puruhit Swami I proposed that we go to India and make a translation that would read as though the original had been written in Common English. (*The Ten Principal Upanishads* 8)

To render the original Sanskrit into "Common English" is indeed a formidable task—next to impossible! There are many translations of the *Upanishads* into English and this is no occasion to discuss this aspect. However, Yeats achieves his objective because he is a poet and he had the guidance of Purohit Swami, collaboration similar to the one between Christopher Isherwood (who, incidentally was also my teacher) and Swami Prabhavananda which resulted in translating Sanskrit religious texts like the *Bhagavad Gita*. It is a pity though, that Yeats could not visit India. Here is his confession:

> When lack of health and money made India impossible we choose Majorca to escape telephones and foul weather,

> and there the work was done, not, as I had planned, in ease and leisure, but in the interstices left me by a long illness. Yet I am satisfied, I have escaped the polyglot, hyphenated, Latinized, muddied muddle of distortion that froze belief. (*The Ten Principal Upanishads* 8)

Yeats was very well instructed by Purohit Swami and this is revealed in his own Preface when he explains:

> Upanishad is doctrine or wisdom (literality 'At the feet of', meaning thereby 'At the feet of some Master') the doctrine or wisdom of the Vedas. Each is attached to some section and sometimes is named from the section. The Katha-Upanishad for instance is part of the 'Katha Brahmana' section in the Yejurveda. (*The Ten Principal Upanishads* 11-12)

All quotations from W.B. Yeats himself have been given here to argue that Yeats's interest in India was intense and genuine. Now we take note of the Indian journey of Yeats.

II

For the framework of the essay four Sanskrit concepts are chosen from the Upanishads. These are *Shreyas*, *Preyas*, *Para* and *Apara*. The first two appear in *Katha Upanishad* and the latter two in *Mundaka Upanishad*. I desist from quoting the original as *Devanagari* script has to be used. Indeed, I give Yeats's own translation of the relevant passages. *Preyas* refers to worldly success and *Shreyas* in pursuit of spiritual progress and wisdom. As Yeats puts it

> The ignorant man runs after pleasure,
> sinks into the entanglements of death; but
> The wise man, seeking the undying, does
> not run away things that die.
>
> (*The Ten Principal Upanishads* 33)

My argument is that Yeats, in his long poetical career progresses from *Preyas* to *Shreyas*. Now the words *Apara* and *Para*. Again Yeats's translation:

> Those who know the spirit that there are two kinds of knowledge, a lower and a higher. The lower is

> the knowledge of the four Vedas and such things as pronunciation, ceremonial, grammar, etymology, poetry, astronomy. The higher knowledge is the knowledge of the Everlasting. (*The Principal Upanishads* 49-50)

Again Yeats's journey is from the former to the latter. This *Knowledge of the Everlasting* started with the poems like, "Lake Isle of Innisfree" and "The Indian Upon God" where he talks of the anthropomorphist idea of God. The journey continues through "Sailing to Byzantium" and "Byzantium" and ends up "Meru". Both Byzantium and Meru attain the status of symbols as we shall see. The interest of Yeats was triggered by his writing the introduction to Bhagavan Sri Hamsa's "The Holy Mountain" and his own rendering of the ten major Upanishads. He translates "Isha" as "The Lord", "Kena" as "At Whose Command", Katha as "From the Katha Branch of the Vedas", "Prasna" as "Questions", "Mudaka" as "At the Feet of the Monk", "Mandookya" as "At the Feet of Master Mandooka", "Taittiriya" as "From the Taittiriya Branch of the Vedas", "Aitareya" as "At the feet of the Master Aitareya", "Chandogya" as "The Doctrine of the Chandogyas" and "Brihdaranyaka" as "Famous Debates in the Forest". Yeats's is an internal spiritual journey from the physical to the metaphysical and there is a period of transition. This transition is through the "Dialogue of self and soul". What Yeats means by Self here refers to the physical and Soul represents the metaphysical. In this poem, the "Dialogue" ends in the Self winning over the Soul which becomes a monologue. My argument is that this is not the end of the journey of Yeats. This is a stage of transition. The voyage of self-discovery makes him sail to Byzantium. The poem "Sailing to Byzantium" should be read in conjunction with the sequel "Byzantium". Sailing is the picture of a voyage from the material world to the holy city of Eternity. "Byzantium" is a vision of the city from the inside. Since it's a personal account I may mention that the experience of the poem came to me in an unusual manner. "Byzantium" explores death and the wisdom of the past. The Goldsmith's art can give the significance of life. Unattainable to what Yeats has called the "Self". The mosaics which depict the spiritual experience are stabilized by the technique of the artist.

The spirits are made triumphant. The personal experience that I referred to is what happened to me on my first visit to Venice. I was sitting in a café at midnight in St. Mark's Square and the gong that was heard transported me. The first few lines of a poem of "Byzantium", suddenly acquired a spiritual meaning through the gradual emptying of the square. In the grand Conch, the gondolas slowly drifting away made me partake in Yeats's beginning lines of the poem. Now we sail away from Byzantium after having sailed to it. The direction we take is on the mountain path to reach "Meru" or "Everest". However, we must stop here for a while. The name "Byzantium" has poetic evocations of Yeats. The name Byzantium was changed to Constantinople and now it has become 'Istanbul'. Istanbul is certainly not Byzantium! Byzantium represents the highest point in the ancient world— the Greek world. Then came the Roman world. That is why in "Meru", Yeats writes, "Egypt and Greece, good bye, and good bye Rome!" Now let me look at the poem "Meru", which according to me, is the final destination of Yeats.

III

Civilization is hoped together, brought
under a rule, under the semblance of peace
By manifold illusion; but man's life is thought
And he, despite his terror, cannot cease
Ravening, raging and uprooting that he may come
into the desolation of reality
Egypt and Greece, good bye, and good bye, Rome!
Hermits upon Mount Meru or Everest
Covered in night under the drifted snow,
Or where that snow and Winter's dreadful blast
Beat down upon their naked bodies, know
That day brings round the night, that before dawn
His glory and the monuments are gone.

To return to the Upanishadic of *Shreyas* and *Paravidya*, "Meru" is the culmination of these concepts. But before exploring the symbolic aspect of "Meru", it is important to mention that it has a Geographic, Pouranic, Legendary, Mythological and Historical background.

> In the Himalayas near *Badarikashrama* is situated Sumeru Mountain. It is also called *Pancha Parvata* because it has five peaks. Rudra Himalaya, Vishnupuri, Brahmapuri, Udgarista and Swargarohini. Four of the five Pandavas died at the last mountain. It is clear that Sumeru Mountain was the place where the Aryans were created. It was the abode of Brahma, Vishnu and Shiva and all the deities. It was the location of Swargaloka. Swayambhu and Vaivaswata Manu lived there. The *Matsya Purana* states that Sumeru Mountain is bounded on the North by Uttara Kuru, on the South by Bharata Varsha, on the West Ketumala mountain and on the East by Bhadrashwa Varsha. The *Padma Purana* mentions that the Ganga arises from the Sumeru Mountain and joins the ocean flowing through Bharata Varsha in the South. A few Aryans migrated from Sumeru Mountain to Mount Meru.

One of the reasons for the present paper is to place the poem "Meru" specifically in the Indian context. The above geographical location of Meru makes it important in the context of Yeats's "Vision" and interest in India. Yeats's interest has shifted from the West by the mention of Greece, Rome and Byzantium to Bharata Varsha, i.e. the East—specifically India.

My argument is that Yeats in "Meru" is specifically exploring the difference between "Manifold illusion" and "desolation of reality". For Yeats who had translated Ten Major Upanishads the Indian metaphysical distinction between illusion and Reality was a Paramount importance. Illusion is "Maya", Reality is "Satta". It is only by giving up all worldly possessions that one can attain the knowledge of Brahman or Ultimate Reality—in fact, the only Reality. This shows that the evolution of Yeats the poet, to Yeats the Philosopher. Illusion belongs to the world of *Preyas* and Reality to *Shreyas*. Manifold illusion is headed away and the core is attained by "hermits" upon Mount Meru or Everest where "Snow and winder's blast beat down upon their naked bodies." As far as Indian readers are concerned Meru is a more potent symbol than Byzantium. To recall our concepts of "Shreyas" and "Para Vidya" Yeats is transcending the "Preyas" and "Apara". There are three kinds of "Satta" or "Reality in Vedanta." The Vyavaharika Satta or Physical Reality, the Pratibhasika Satta or illusion such as mistaking the rope for a serpent and Paramarthika Satta or the One, unchanging, eternal, non-dual (Advaitic) Reality enshrined in the concept of Brahman. My argument has been that Yeats has moved from the first to the third level in his long career as a poet. We end as we began with Yeats's translation of another "Shanti Mantra":

> That is perfect, this is perfect
> Perfect comes from Perfect.
> Take perfect from perfect, the remainder is perfect.
> (*The Ten Principal Upanishads* 15)

Works Cited

Reine, Kathreen. *Yeats the Initiate: Essays on Certain Themes in the Work of W.B. Yeats*. London: George Allen and Unwin Limited, 1986. Print.

Yeats, W.B. *The Ten Principal Upanishads*. London: Faber and Faber, 1937. Print.

——. "Meru", *W.B. Yeats: Selected Poems*. Ed. Webb, Trimothy. London: Penguin Books, 1991. Print.

Ranganath, S. (Unpublished Paper). "Migration of Aryans According to Purans".

5

'A Woman Lost': A Reading of the Maud Gonne Poems of Yeats

C.T. Indra

A poet often constructs his own system based on his value system, his priorities and prejudices. Invariably, it is rooted in a cultural milieu. By a conscious effort where he constructs a system of values and beliefs, which he tries to incarnate in myths and symbols, he invests the system with a referentiality. Although it may not be valid in universal terms, it is interpretable within the system.

W.B. Yeats was particularly adept in constructing such systems. Although there are a number of prominent images and symbols in the poetry of Yeats, there is one bright constellation having at its centre the figure of Maud Gonne supported by certain other figures which are recurrent. Together they constitute a system of signs reflecting on the poet's changing role in his society. Whether Maud Gonne may be best regarded as an icon or index or a sign is a difficult question to answer. The following study aims to show that in Yeats's poetry, she partakes of the attributes of all the three. The complication of the system is to be understood in terms of the tension Yeats felt between his conservative aristocratic values and the feeling of rationalism which Maud Gonne inspired in him. The love of his culture prompted him to

This is the revised and expanded version of the article first published in *Scholastic International Journal of Language and Literature,* Vol. I, Issue 3, Sept. 2011: 83-96 (brought out by the Ethiraj College for Women, Chennai).

be involved in the Irish National Movement. But the vulgarity and coarseness of politics repelled him. His problem, in brief, was how to touch pitch and yet not get defiled. His impression of Maud Gonne at first served to give him a clue. She was in the thick of violent politics, and yet she seemed a glorious figure untouched by dross. However, the poet became aware of a deeper level where there was an inevitable ambivalence. He gave superb articulation to this ambivalence through exploiting the figure of Maud Gonne.

W.B. Yeats asks in his poignant reflection on old age in the poem "The Tower":

> Does the Imagination dwell the most
> Upon a woman won or woman lost?

The poet's passion and his unrequited love for Maud Gonne, who was a political leader in the Irish National Movement, are well chronicled not only by his biographers, but by his own poetic oeuvre. There are innumerable references to Maud Gonne, either direct or implied, all over his poetry, not to mention whole pieces reflecting on his strange passion for 'a proud woman not kindred of his soul', as he put it in "The Dialogue of Self and Soul". Although it is not uncommon for poets to make a fetish of their love, the uniqueness of Yeats's love for Maud Gonne is that the man's loss was the poet's gain. Maud Gonne indeed assumes an iconic dimension through the course of Yeats's development as a poet and emerges as a rich symbol in his creative output.

Yeats met Maud Gonne first in 1889, introduced by John O'Leary when his first book of poems *The Wanderings of Oison* was published. He was 23 and he fell in love with Maud Gonne at first sight. She was British, a Colonel's daughter, but deeply involved in the Irish struggle for freedom. In fact, she was responsible for the poet Yeats to actively engage himself in politics, at least for some time. "Did I tell you how much I admire Miss Gonne? She will make many converts to her political belief" (Untrecker 12). However, he could not see eye to eye with her on many political issues. He was much too aristocratic to concede to the force of vulgarity. "The seeming needs of my fool-driven land" tempted him "from the craft of verse", he wrote in the poem "All Things can Tempt Me" (*Collected Poems* 109). On her part she wanted his poetry to serve the cause of Irish culture and politics. She had early declared "The world will thank me for not marrying you, but do go on writing me these wonderful poems" (qtd. in *W.B. Yeats*, A.N. Jeffares 17). Yeats courted her unsuccessfully for thirteen years and ended when she married Major John MacBride in 1903. Maud Gonne's political career was not a bed of roses. The same crowd, which she roused to heroic heights, also sneered at her later. Maud Gonne "became ideal beauty in service of an unworthy cause" (Untrecker 13). Yeats wrote, "She had to choose (perhaps all women must) between broomstick and distaff and she has chosen the broomstick—I mean the witches' hats" (Untrecker 13). Maud Gonne was converted to Catholicism and hence could not divorce MacBride, although she separated from him. Yeats's courtship might have ended, but his passion was not entirely 'barren'. Yeats's poetry found one of its 'masterful images' in the person of Maud Gonne.

II

Maud Gonne is apotheosized in several ways in Yeats's poetry. She is transported in some of the poems to the Celtic past and assumes protean shapes and significances. She becomes Cathleen, daughter of Houlihan, a heroic figure who sacrificed her life for the sake of her country and her people. She becomes, in effect, the symbol of Ireland, that Ireland which the poet wishes to see in its glory. In that sense, it is almost an unattainable ideal. In his play *Cathleen Ni Houlihan* (1902), Yeats depicted her as an old woman but one capable of regeneration. Maud Gonne herself played the role of Cathleen (with her erect, proud demeanour that Yeats was never tired of admiring). The merging of the images of Countess Cathleen and Maud Gonne and Yeats's life-long ambivalent response to this composite picture, finds agonizing expression in stanza III of his last poem of self-assessment, "Circus Animals' Desertion" (Countess Cathleen was 'pity-crazed' and would have 'given her soul away'). But she was redeemed by Heaven. Her temperament and predicament sadly remind the poet of Maud Gonne. Alas! He could not prevail upon her to give up the ways of violence, but the wracking of his heart wrung poetry from his soul:

> I thought my dear must her own soul destroy.
> So did fanaticism and hate enslave it.
> And this brought forth a dream and soon enough
> This dream itself had all my thought and love.
> ("The Circus Animals' Desertion", *Collected Poems* 392)

In the pre-Raphaelite volume *The Rose* (1893) Yeats uses the Rose at once as an emblem of Maud Gonne and Ireland. To the young poet, in love with her, the Rose was the hope of the future, although his people are at present demoralized.

The cult of heroism finds superb expression in poem after poem wherein Yeats images Maud Gonne as Helen of Troy and occasionally as Pallas Athene. The Helen motif is part of a cluster of images in Yeats's poetry, symbolizing heroism, which, he believes, no longer exists in the sordid modern world where people

> ...fumble in a greasy till
> And add the half-penny to the penny
> And prayer to shivering prayer, until
> you have dried the marrow from the bone.
> ("September 1913", *Collected Poems* 120)

Helen of Troy invokes associations of a grand civilization, though doomed to fall. Maud Gonne thus assumes a mythological dimension.

A series of poems in the volume *Green Helmet and Other Poems* published in 1910 harp on this idea. "A Woman Homer Sung" is a poem of three stanzas of seven lines each. The poet is already the loser in the pursuit of love. In stanza I, he recalls to himself his youthful pining for her. In stanza II, he tells us how this love inspired his poetry and spurred his creative imagination ("I wrote and wrought"). Like Shakespeare in his sonnets to the young man, Yeats knows that he had brought his passion to such a pitch that the coming time can say.

> He shadowed in the glass
> What thing her body was.
> ("A Woman Homer Sung", *Collected Poems* 100)

The poet is aware that the man's loss is the poet's gain. In the last stanza he realizes that she was not just any woman but had 'fiery blood' while he was treading on a cloud. She was a 'woman Homer sung'. She had become the very embodiment of 'an heroic dream'.

"No Second Troy" which follows just a poem later in the volume, is bitter and sardonic, expressing disgust, not only with himself but also with the whole shoddy political atmosphere. The incongruity between Maud Gonne's heroic dream and the sordid state of affairs in contemporary Ireland is reiterated all through the poem. He tells himself in disgust that he won't chide her for teaching.

> ...ignorant men most violent ways.
> Or hurled the little streets upon the great.
>
> ("No Second Troy", *Collected Poems* 109)

He is full of contempt for those who have no 'courage equal to desire' in sharp contrast she is:

> nobleness made simple as a fire,
> With beauty like a tightened bow
> That is not natural in an age like this
> Being high and solitary and most stern?
>
> ("No Second Troy", *Collected Poems* 109)

The image of the tightened bow is not only arresting, capturing the erect posture of Maud Gonne which Yeats often refers to, but it also symbolizes the upright heroism which is not 'natural in an age like this'. How does the 'tightened bow' become a loaded image? By the way, Yeats charges it with a stern heroism. It comes to stand for a whole age, a whole civilization. It projects an image of Man ready for action. It symbolizes 'courage equal to desire'. The 'fire' is another recurrent word associated with Maud Gonne and her kind. It stands for a heroic passion which burns all the dross. Fire also prepares us for the last line

> Was there another Troy for her to burn?

This is an ambivalent question, though normally speaking all rhetorical questions should have a simple answer. Here on the surface of it, the suggestion is that we are no more living in heroic times when a whole city could be burnt down for a sake of a beautiful woman. But there is also an implied apprehension that Maud Gonne's passion might after all be unnatural, ill-directed, destructive. Hence, the complex of beauty and heroism, especially of the sterile kind (later reflected upon in "Easter 1916"), is accurately captured by the series Helen, Troy, fire and tightened bow.

The same ambivalent marks another poem "Against Unworthy Praise". The poet is here sermonizing to himself: he says that the fact that the 'knave or dolt' cannot appreciate his poetry need not deter him. For he wrote his poems for a 'woman's sake'. She could make 'dream that lion dreamed'. Being proud herself she could kindle the pride in him. Then his mind turns to what happened to her own case. She gave so much to the people, but she earned

> ...slander, ingratitude,
> From self-same dolt and knave.
>
> ("Against Unworthy Praise", *Collected Poems* 104)

The poet grants, in fairness, that is surely a greater irony. Yet she is not broken. She still cheerfully caries on:

> Yet she, singing upon her road
> Half-lion, half-child, is at peace.
>
> ("Against Unworthy Praise", *Collected Poems* 104)

The image of the lion repeated throughout the poem joins the cluster of images constituting heroism which transcends time and place. It is set off by the repetition of the unheroic 'dolt' (i.e., 1.2 and 1.17). However, even this is not without a tinge of ambivalence for the poet marks a certain strangeness in her which 'perplexes'. The syntax of that line is ambiguous. If 'perplexed' used as an intransitive verb or as a participle?

> But here's the haughtier text,
> The labyrinth of her days
> That her own strangeness perplexed
>
> ("Against Unworthy Praise", *Collected Poems* 104)

Does the 'haughtier text' refer to Maud Gonne's own life, herself? Is it described as 'the labyrinth', suggesting elaborate, laborious effort and also having an enigma at the centre? Did the labyrinth of her days perplex her own strangeness? If so, 'perplex' is used transitively.

The irreconcilability of fact and reality is stressed by the words 'dreams', 'dreamed', and 'dreaming'.

There is, however, one divergent note in the next volume *Responsibilities* (1914). In the poem "When Helen Lived" the poet seems to ruminate on the fatal charm of beauty. He seems to realize that even in those days when 'Helen walked with her boy', 'within/ those topless towers', the men and women of Troy must have thought of it as a jest, a 'trivial affair'. Does the poet mean to say that the world has not changed at all since the time of the Trojan War?

But the poem "Fallen Majesty" goes back to the tone of "No Second Troy". The difference lies here. The poet has once again recovered his faith in heroism and the cult of heroism. The bitterness of tone in the poem is caused by the unworthiness of the common rabble, 'the crowd' for whom Maud Gonne gave all her life's energy. With his wonted self-irony, the poet describes his own devotion to her in mediaeval feudal terms as that of "some last courtier at a gypsy camping place/ Babbling of fallen majesty". The heroism of Maud Gonne is transubstantiated into a 'burning cloud'. The ethereal beauty and aura of Maud Gonne are captured in the lines

> A crowd
> Will gather, and not know it walks the very street
> Whereon a thing once walked that seemed a
> burning cloud.

("Fallen Majesty", *Collected Poems* 138)

Ezra Pound altered the line as

> "Once walked a thing that seemed a burning cloud."

because he wanted to remove tautology. Although Yeats accepted the revision in part, he rendered it finally as

> "Whereas a thing once walked that seemed a burning cloud."

Yeats's intention was to keep the metrical pattern intact. Modernist critics like C.K. Stead have criticized. Yeats for surrendering clarity and hardness to rhetoric and incantation (*Pound, Yeats and Eliot and the Modernist Movement* 22ff.). The point is that the title "Fallen Majesty" and the poem are a part of a semiotic system constituted by Helen, Troy, Homer, dream, lion, fire, tightened bow and burning cloud. The poet is the bard who sings,

> I record what's gone.

He will tell the world of the rise and fall of this regal beauty. She is seen at once as a symbol and as part of a vast cyclic movement of history.

Hence, when we move to the poem "Leda and the Swan" (in the *Tower* Volume of 1928), its iconic effect and its quality of being a spectacle (i.e. a temporal history frozen in a spatial image) strikes us most. It describes Jove's raping of Leda, Helen's mother, and its consequences for Western civilization. In the first stanza, the focus is on the strangely sensual scene depicting the helplessness of a girl caught in a violent, compulsive act of seduction by a bird. Stanza II diverts our attention from the rape to the surrender of the girl ('Loosening thighs', 'laid in that white rush'). She now becomes a passive receptacle of the 'feathered glory' which is none other than Jove who came in the form of a swan. Stanza III suddenly moves from the fanciful to the historical, by simply alluding to the Trojan War by Agamemnon, the broken all, the burning roof and the tower. Once again the Helen motif looms large. The rape of Leda engendered a Helen whose fatal beauty, in turn, engendered the Trojan War, resulting in the destruction of the city.

The last stanza poses a rhetorical question (as does "No Second Troy") and brings the poem to an ambivalent close. The poet wonders how someone like Helen could have helped being what she was, being the daughter of the 'brute blood of the air' (*Collected Poems* 241)? The poet speculates whether

her mother Leda put on Jove's knowledge with his power. By describing Jove's state of mind after the rape by the synecdoche 'the indifferent beak', the poet perhaps suggests that civilizations cannot help being raised only to be razed down by man's passion and indifference.

"Leda and the Swan" does not directly allude to Maud Gonne. But the recurrent Helen of Troy motif, exploited at the level of a historical vision, compels us to see Maud Gonne as a part of the whole thought process. No doubt the poet is distanced from his usual passion. He is envisioning the birth and destruction of a civilization with a detachment that he will much more superbly command in his last poems. In one such poem "The Long-Legged Fly", the poet once again goes back to the burning of Troy and Helen, and this for the last time.

> That topless towers be burnt
> And men recall that face,
> Move most gently if move you must,
> In this lonely place.
>
> She thinks part woman three parts a child,
> That nobody looks; her feet
> Practise a tinker shuffle
> Picked up on a street.
>
> Like a long-legged fly upon the stream
> Her mind moves upon silence.
>
> ("The Long-Legged Fly", *Collected Poems* 381)

The opening lines of the stanza, of course recall Marlowe's superb invocation to Helen in *Dr. Faustus*. There she was a phantom. Here she is an enigma. She is both a woman and a child (recalling the line 'half-lion, half-child is at peace' in "Against Unworthy Praise"). She is caught in a characteristic activity even as, in stanzas I and III, Julius Caesar and Michaelangelo are. While Caesar is intently gazing on a map in a military camp. Michaelangelo is reclining on his scaffolding, painting the first Adam on the roof of the Sistine Chapel. Helen is practicing a shuffle like a girl. All of them are sculpted with an artist's detachment by the poet. There is a recognition of the inevitability of each person's genius and its cosmic purpose especially if he/ she has a public role of perform. The tone of the poet's voice is calm, all passion spent. The long-legged fly, sitting motionless on the moving stream, symbolizes at once the poet's detachment and the inevitability of the movement of Time, carrying individuals on its stream.

Thus prepared, we go to the very last poem Yeats wrote exclusively on Maud Gonne: "A Bronze Head". In this poem, she has been transformed from a thing of the life and blood into a work of art and become part of the 'artifice of eternity'. Stanza I leads us into the art gallery. We are arrested by 'this broze head' (another powerful use of the deictic 'this' as the 'that' in "Sailing to Byzantium"). It is both human and super-human. Maud Gonne has always been associated with a bird-like beauty (compare 'the Ledaean body' in "Among School Children"). Now her eye resembles a bird's round eye and stands out prominently against the rest of the body which has withered and is mummy-like. She becomes a 'great tomb-haunter'. She has gone beyond life into the realm of death. Yet she seems to hover over the sky like those huge predatory birds as if some longing of hers is not yet satisfied. The poem reminds us of "No Second Troy", when the poet wonders if the hysteria which propelled her all her life has now increased or emptied itself, finding nothing to equal her passion. The allusion to King Lear and his heroic effort to smother his 'hysterico passio' cannot go unnoticed. Yeats had said in "A Prayer for My Daughter",

> It's certain that fine women eat
> A crazy salad with their meat
> Whereby the Horn of Plenty is undone.
>
> (*Collected Poems* 212)

The language here is deliberately banal whereas in "A Bronze Head" it is sublime.

Stanza II becomes a bit touching when it moves back from art to life, recalling her form

...all full
As though with magnanimity of light,
Yet a most gentle woman.

("A Bronz Head", *Collected Poems* 382)

The poet soon recovers his detachment and contemplates on the mystery of human personality and thinks of philosophers' opinion on this matter. In humanity, he recognizes that it is well nigh impossible to say which of her forms has shown her substance right. Was she a crazy woman? Was she a child? He remembers how there was a streak of 'wildness' in her (St. III), and the poet regretted how a 'vision of terror' must inevitably 'shatter her soul'. The poet was moved to pity that someone, so remarkably gifted, should be so fatally drawn to wilderness. Hence he murmurs "My child, my child!"

From another angle, perhaps, it was equally true that she was not just crazy but 'supernatural' (St. IV) who gauged rightly this 'foul world in its decline and fall'. She might have decided to act crazy since

On gangling stocks grown great, great stocks
run dry,
Ancestral pearls all pitched into a sky,
Heroic reverie mocked by clown and knave.

("A Bronz Head", *Collected Poems* 383)

Not having another Troy to burn, she might have wondered:

...what was left for massacre to save.

(*Collected Poems* 383)

The poem's end is ambivalent, wistful, perhaps in an aristocratic way looking with withering contempt at this vulgar world. He seems to want to endorse Maud Gonne's opinion that the world no more is worthy of heroic ideals. And yet the poet has come a long way. His own passion for the woman is spent and transformed into, to be precise an aesthetician's perception. He calmly contemplates the woman as an object of art and endeavours to decipher the reality it points to. The poet is preoccupied with its mystery, its polysemy.

We have only to compare this poem with "A Prayer for My Daughter" from the volume *Michael Robartes and the Dancer* (1921) to see how Yeats was constantly trying to transmute personal emotions into detached reflections on human nature and the destiny of cultures. "A Prayer for My Daughter" is a fine reflection on the propensities of female nature and the poet is neither hysterical nor sentimental about it. He wishes that his daughter would cherish 'custom and ceremony' so that she may avoid the failings of a Maud Gonne. There is, in the poem, a somber stanza on the consequences for the soul if it allowed 'intellectual hatred' to influence it. There is here an allusion to Maud Gonne, when once again using rhetorical syntax, Yeats asks,

> Have I not seen the loveliest woman born
> Out of the mouth of Plenty's horn,
> Because of her opinionated mind
> Batter that horn and every good
> By quiet natures understood
> For an old bellows full of angry wind?

(*Collected Poems* 213)

In this poem, 'intellectual hatred' is contrasted with 'radical innocence', which we learn is 'self-delighting', 'self-appeasing' and 'self-affrighting' (*Collected Poems* 214). Yeats sees Maud Gonne as one driven too far by her political ideas, thereby destroying the inner beauty of her being. The image of cornucopia is a symbol of abundance, fullness which Maud Gonne seems to have spurned. The poet also realizes that Maud Gonne could not have helped it. Hence, he says,

> Helen being chosen found life flat and dull.

(*Collected Poems* 212)

When we have looked at the whole complex system of Maud Gonne and the Helen of Troy references, we may formulate our responses in the following way:

The poet conceives of his function as an image maker and his role is to examine his society, culture and history and civilization at large and he does it chiefly as a bard. With the eye of a visionary he creates symbols out of all kinds of sources he fancies, depending on his taste and priorities. He constructs a value-system in terms of those symbols. The symbols are not one-dimensional to be sure. They are not without referentiality either. Polysemy is not a matter of fancy, but is the result of the ambivalence in the poet's attitude to his theme.

The style of Yeats undergoes remarkable changes and the poems studied are indices to the way the best in the modes of Pre-Raphaelitism, Symbolism and Imagism are assimilated by the articulate energy of this poet. The group of poems involving Maud Gonne, thus, gain referentiality at several levels. At the most personal level they reflect Yeats's struggle to overcome his passion for a woman whom he could not win. At the level of poetic spiritual autobiography, it reflects his ability not only to make poetry out of his suffering ("We make out of our quarrel with others, rhetoric, but of our quarrel with ourselves poetry", said Yeats in "Anima Hominis"), but develop a network of symbols and images. This is made possible by his ability to transcend the personal and achieve an aesthetic distance. His passion is transmuted by his poetic energy. In fact, it sustains it all through his life. One may even say that more than Byzantium or the Tower, the image of Maud Gonne accounts for a variety of poems ranging from the personal to the political, from the fanciful to the mythological. Frank Kermode has studied in his book *Romantic Image* Yeats's search for a dynamic or living beauty. In some ways Maud Gonne served such a need in Yeats's poetic development. At the most general level the range of stylistic variation among the Maud Gonne poems reflects on the course of development that English poetry took, from the days of Pre-Raphaelitism (with its exquisiteness as well as effete romanticism) through Symbolism (with its moments of magical revelation and esoteric imagery) till the crystallization of Modernism in the second and third decades of the twentieth century (when poetic idiom registered a radical break with the immediate past and moved towards a greater hardness and spareness). Yeats's poetry is an index to this aspect of contemporary poetic history. The Maud Gonne poems illustrate practically all the experiments that marked the thirty years from 1890-1920.

Works Cited

Finneran, R.J., G.M. Harper and William Murray, Eds. *Letters of W.B. Yeats*. Vol. I, London: Macmillan, 1977. Print.

Jeffares, A.N. *W.B. Yeats*, Profiles in Literature Series. London: Routledge, 1971. Print.

——. *W.B. Yeats: Man and the Poet*, 1949. London: Routledge, 1978. Print.

Kermode, Frank. *Romantic Image*. London: Routledge, 2nd ed. 2001. Print.

Stead, C.K. *Pound, Yeats and Eliot and the Modernist Movement*. Palgrave Macmillan, 1986. Print.

Untrecker, John. *A Reader's Guide to W.B. Yeats*. London: James and Hudson, 1959. Print.

W.B. Yeats. *The Collected Poems of W.B. Yeats*. London: Macmillan, 1963.

6

The Poetry of Unageing Intellect

Prabhat K. Singh

The poetry of W.B. Yeats, the Nobel Laureate, is a fascinating work of "unageing intellect". T.S. Eliot rightly considered him 'always a contemporary'. The large canvas of his creative writing reflects the intellectual robustness and wide horizon of his mind enriched by his encounters with a variety of truths and his intense involvement in the activities of institutions like Dublin Hermatic Society, Madame Blavatsky's Theosophical Society, the Rhymers' Club, and the Irish Theatrical Society popularly known as Abbey Theatre. His associations with celebrated literary personalities like William Morris and Burne Jones, the Pre-Raphaelites, George Russell, his friend and co-founder of the Hermetic Society, Oscar Wilde and R.L. Stevenson, his co-founders of the Rhymers' Club, Arthur Symons who introduced him to French symbolism and aestheticism of Mallarme, Baudelaire and Verlaine, and George Moore and Ezra Pound who helped him modernize his style, are highly significant. Besides, Parnell and John O'Leary, the guiding spirits of Irish Renaissance, Lady Gregory, his patron, and Maud Gonne, the nationalist and his beloved paragon of beauty, are inseparable from his consciousness. The hereditary gain from his father, John Butler Yeats, a painter, an intellectual, a skeptic, an agnostic and a wit, is also undeniable. It was his father who initiated him into the poetry of Rossetti and Blake at the age of sixteen. Above all, his studies of spiritualism, magic and occult sciences, theosophy, esoteric Buddhism and the secret lore of Cabbala were further enriched by his interaction with

Rabindranath Tagore, Purohit Swamy and Mohini Chatterjee, the Vedantees.

Progressing through the imagist and symbolist movements, Yeats's poetic career charts the course of the development of poetry from the naughty nineteen to the first three decades of the twentieth century. His career is divided into five phases—the first phase from 1885 to 1902, the second from 1903 to 1914, the third from 1915 to 1928, the fourth from 1928 to 1935 and the last phase from 1935 to 1939. His poems are published in fourteen volumes: *Crossways* (1889), *The Rose* (1893), *The Wind Among the Reeds* (1899), *In the Seven Woods* (1904), *The Green Helmet and Other Poems* (1910), *Responsibilities* (1914), *The Wild Swans at Coole* (1919), *Michael Robartes and the Dancer* (1921), *The Tower* (1928), *The Winding Stair and Other Poems* (1933), *Words for Music Perhaps, A Woman Young and Old, A Full Moon in March* (1935), and *Last Poems* (1936-39).

Yeats's early poetry of the Celtic twilight period is frankly escapist. It is pre-Raphaelitic and romantic. His youthful imagination nourished on the poetry of Spenser, Shelley, Blake and Keats, and his seeking in the self and assimilation of the whole universe put him firmly in the romantic tradition. His choice of the common speech for the language of poetry is Wordsworthian. Besides, Shelleyan fluidity and Keatsean richness of colour mark the texture of his verse. He began very much like Keats as an adolescent aesthete feeling out of gear with the unshapely realities of the actual world. This left him with two options, either to escape into the world of Irish myths and legends, as he does, for example, in his poem, "The Stolen Child":

> Come away, O human child!
> To the waters and the wild
> With a faery hand in hand,
> For the world's more full of weeping than you
> Can understand. (Yeats 5)

or to refashion to shut his own aesthetic disposition, as done, for example, in "The Lover Tells of the Rose in His Heart":

> The wrong of unshapely things is a wrong too great to be told;
> I hunger to build them anew and sit on a green knoll apart,
> With the earth and the sky and the water, re-made, like a casket of gold
> For my dreams of your image that blossoms a rose in the deeps of my heart. (Yeats 25)

The dream world of Irish legends, myths and folklore this inspires the raptures of the young poet's early poetry. He lives much in fairlyland and his heroes, Oisin Red, Hanrahan, always desert the real world. "The Lake Isle of Innisfree", "The Man who Dreamed of Fairy Land" and "The Stolen Claw" are his finest escape poems presenting a world of vague and dim landscape with uncertain half-lights and blurred outlines, a world in which everyday a twilight sheds with fantastic effects. The style of the early poetry is easy and languid weighted with clotty metaphors and epithets and showing the influence of Spenser, Shelley, Keats, Tennyson, Swinburne and the Pre-Raphaelites. It is highly coloured, but the colours are pale, shadowy and misty in keeping with the vague, wistful and nostalgic tone.

However, his dream poetry contains the germs of his later poetry. Innisfree is not merely a dream world but also an actual island opposite to Sligo that was familiar to Yeats since his childhood. Yeats' love of Irish peasantry and his treatment of history, legend and folklore also serves the patriotic purpose of reviving the ancient culture by Irish stories and tales of heroism. Real rivers, mountains and valleys appear repeatedly and bring the escape poetry into a lively contact with reality. This forms the familiar Yeatsean antithesis between the world of imagination and the world of facts, between sustained vision (art and mythology) and time and chance, between, what Yeats calls, the province of soul and the province of heart. In addition, the very urge to escape into the world of peace and shelter shows his awareness of the inadequacies of reality, its conflicts and machinations. Thus, the core of reality in his early poetry foreshadows the realism of his poetry to come. The two are also interrelated as bringing together of opposites is the keynote of Yeats's poetry. Yeats transfers ancient myths and legends into a modern context and creates new myths out of the old ones thus giving them a new significance. As a result, while the Irish legends clustering round Oisin, Fergus and the like retain their individual characters, they also mirror the poet's personality. This experimentation with somewhat unfamiliar frames of reference brings Yeats close to William Blake who developed a private mythology with deities and angels such as Los, Val, Urizen who were strange to the people for they mostly thought of Mercury, Vulcan or Zeus as Gods.

Yeats soon grows out of the exotic, fairy-haunted world of his youth. Before his final transition to life and reality takes place, there follows a brief phase in which he makes a voyage within withdrawing as much as possible from the contemporary world and enriching his inner life by concentrating on purely visionary themes. Under the influence of the French symbolists and the English aesthetes—Mallarme, Arthus Symons and Walter Pater—he accepts the conception of pure poetry and adoration of beauty, although Mallarme's theories are too abstract to match Yeats's passionate disposition. Having learnt from Mallarme and other symbolists that absolute beauty could be created only by using symbols, he makes persistent use of highly individual and complex symbols. Besides, believing in the theory of 'art for art's sake', he writes pure poetry. However, his poem, "In the Seven Woods", marks a turning point in his career as he strikes a new note of sharp satire and realism in it. After making his voyage within and discovering the beauty, which he found terrible and inhuman:

> All changed, changed utterly;
> A terrible beauty is born. (Yeats 93)

he comes out of his ivory tower and connects himself with the harsh realities of life. In his poem, "In Memory", which commemorates a public personality, Yeats's ideological world is shaken by the bitter winds of reality and change. The poem shimmers with a profound sense of disquietude. In brief, his frustration in love, his bitter experiences in politics and in the Abbey Theatre, his involvement in public controversies—all combine to shatter his illusion and produce the harsh sardonic tone of the poems of this realistic transitional phase. His dreams are gone and he comes closer to life and reality and is conscious of blood and mire and degradation of body. In brief, the changes begins with "In the Seven Woods" and the scope of his subject gradually expands till "The Responsibility". Instead of the remote Greek myths and legends, he creates new myths out of the patriots of the eighteenth century Ireland who still live in the popular imagination.

The change in subject matter corresponds to the change in his style also. The decorative images and languid rhythms are replaced by definite and precise images and the tendency to use the common idiom, the colloquial diction and the speech rhythms, choppy and harsh. In his well-known poem, "A Coat", he presents his ideal of the language of poetry of this period. He discards his coat of rich embroidery "For there is more enterprise/ In walking naked" (Yeats 63). Now his poetic language is shorn of all kinds of decoration. Coming closure to life, he shows intense awareness of external realities in his poetry. The Easter Rebellion, The Civil War, the turmoil in Ireland and Europe, the contemporary personalities, heroes and martyrs (Pears Connolly, MacBride) figure increasingly in his compositions instead of the earlier legendary figures. He thus succeeds in creating new poetical myths out of the contemporary politics and events, which were inspired by Parnell and sustained by John O'Leary and many other Irish patriots and politicians. Yeats's Irishness also takes a new turn when he becomes actively involved in the Irish rebellion of 1913. The rose of art, beauty and love, which had become the rose of passion when he fell in love with Maud Gonne, acquired another shade with the growth of his patriotic fervour. Dreams were undone and hope reduced to futility when the Irish uprising was crushed under the cruel heals of British imperialism. Yeats's disillusionment and his sense of utter futility are vividly captured in his poem, "An Irish Airman Foresees His Death":

> I balanced all, brought all to mind,
> The years to come seemed waste of breath,
> A waste of breath the years behind
> In balance with this life, this death. (Yeats 69)

The awareness of the negative is quite pervasive in this poem of sixteen lines with eight negative implications. The fragmented and passionless character of the country culture finds an impassioned and prophetic expression in it. His "The Second Coming" is closer in spirit to T.S. Eliot's *The Waste Land*, although the powerful passionate quality:

> Things fall apart; the centre cannot hold;
> Mere anarchy is loosed upon the world,
> The blood-dimmed tide is loosed and everywhere
> The ceremony of innocence is drowned. (Yeats 99)

of Yeats's poem sets it apart. Yeats's dealing with the supernatural (through his wife as a medium) enriches his poetry with esoteric symbols such as the wheel, the winding and the gyres. With the traumatic experiences of 'Easter 1916' and the awareness of the common nightmare of the time in "Meditations in Time of Civil War" in the poet's mind, "The Second Coming" is the result of Yeats's contemplation of the idea of balancing violent destruction by equally monstrous rebirth. The archetypal, stone image of Sphinax lying motionless for two thousand years at Giza in Egypt becomes suddenly alive and moves towards Bethlehem, the place of its nativity. The Sphinx is the symbol of intellect and the artist has successfully tried to unite it with emotion to anticipate a new epiphany.

The change in Yeats's style is also related to his disappointment in love. Maud Gonne's marriage to Major John MacBride gives a terrible deathblow to his hopes. Moon embittered, he turns to drama, strips away the elaborate, ornate imagery with which he had decorated his early love poems, and begins to write harder, terser and more epigrammatic poems dealing mainly with politics and metaphysics. His style becomes more dramatic, more precise and more conversational. His involvement in the management of characters helped him in counterbalancing his mysticism and dreaminess and in rooting his work deeply in reality, which he considers the ultimate source of art. However, Maud Gonne remains in his creative consciousness constantly and fruitfully, as the answer is implied in his question:

> Does the imagination dwell the most
> Upon a woman won or woman lost? (Yeats 109)

Yeats's attitude to life in his later poetry is complex. He is bitterly disillusioned, wants to escape from the blood and mire and the degradation of the body and seeks a safe anchorage in the Tower or in Byzantium. Assailed by the apprehension that time and age are nibbling at the passion and power that constituted the foundation heads of his poetry, he develops ambivalence between his love for art and the inevitable decay brought by time and age. This generates the tension between hopes and fears that produces his celebrated poems like "The Tower", "Among School Children", "Leda and the Swan" and "Sailing to Byzantium", to mention a few. "The Tower" opens his most mature poetic phase. Giving a deep sense of rootedness to Yeats, the Tower at Thoor Ballylee becomes a symbol of intellectual glory. Yeats's speculative imagination is here replaced by his confessional intensity and meditative self-absorption. Walking on the pavement of his Tower, he appears more vigorous than earlier. "Among School Children" may be taken as the poet's statement on the ultimate nature of reality: that life is at once changing and changeless, but always unified. The poet's awareness of approaching death makes him nostalgic and consequently injects youthful vigour and vitality into the veins of his poetry. "Leda and the Swan", which presents Yeats's interpretation of the Greek myth about the rape of Leda by Zeus, deals with the dynamic idea of development and fulfillment. The creative power of the Swan flows into the womb of Leda and gives birth to the figures of love and war (Helen and Clytemnestra). The emotional vitality of youth and the intellectual maturity of the old age thus meet and merge in one entity. And in "Sailing to Byzantium", Yeats wishes to assume the form of an immortal piece of art, "a form as Grecian goldsmiths make" (Yeats 105). This wish to move away from the finite and temporal world of the dying generations to the world of the infinite and the eternal also reflects the doctrine of necessary isolation and suffering in the artist. However, his lust for life is equally intense and he is content to live this repeatedly, for he is conscious of the fact that despite the passions being out of tune with modern realities, form and passion are indispensable for a poetic sensibility. Thus, he balances the richness of life against the timelessness of art. To him, art is but a vision of reality and it is, perhaps, more alive than the living, and intellect and spirit are more dependable than blood and mire. Ezra Pound observes the world of natural beings and the world of human artifacts with delicacy and justness, Yeats cares more for poetry than for his own reputation as a poet. Eliot admires Yeats for this attitude; for the integrity of his passion for his art and craft; for considering art greater than the artist. Simultaneously, being innately Romantic (Yeats claimed that he was one of 'the last Romantics'), he keeps frowning at the age of despair and disillusionment. Therefore, there is paradoxical vitality and complexity of moods and tones in his poetry. This complexity produces the rich and magnificent poems of his later phase. His art and technique is now mature. The structure of his poem, "No Second Troy" is bony and bare, but the image pattern is complex and rich. That is why the poems of this period exhibit an astonishing richness and enduring quality. However, the common idiom, the colloquial diction and the speech rhythms of the middle period are still used. But in poems like "Sailing to Byzantium", an effect of rare richness is produced by relating daily speech to an incantatory pattern. Glittering sonorous epithets are now used alternately with choppy words conveying an impression of the stresses and accents of the present reality as also of the mystery and richness of the past.

At every stage of his development, Yeats uses symbols, which he conceives as 'heraldic'. He calls them 'a transparent lamp about a spiritual flame'. Symbols in his poetry are the expressions of some invisible essence. Yeats maintains the concreteness of his symbols as opposed to the French symbolists whose literal objects dissolve in their symbols and disappear. He always seeks to fuse together the physical and the symbolic aspects effectively. His poetry grows through experiments and gradually attains mature symbolic expression. In the early poems, he uses vague and beautiful images of flowers, stars, birds and mythical figures as an escape from the ugliness of the age. In the middle period, his symbolism is more complex, and contemporary personalities are used as symbols of his revolutionary idealism. Now he creates highly complex and intricate symbols personal and new as well as traditional and evocative. The "Lapis Lazuli", which he received as a gift, the "Sword of Sato", "The Tower", and many such personal properties become symbols. He also uses drunkards and lechers—Crazy Jane and Tom the lunatic—as realistic symbols to express his contempt of ugliness and vulgarity. In his later poetry, rich and intricate patterns are presented by bringing together new modes of feeling and expression, new waves of emotion and thought and the linking together of the past and the present and the personal and the impersonal. Symbols enrich the complexity of his later meditative poems. His symbols are essentially dynamic, growing, changing, acquiring greater intensity, depth and density. His interest in Irish myths and folklore, music and magic, philosophy and metaphysics, and paintings and drawings condition his choice of symbols. He makes his 'Tower', or the 'Winding Stair', a permanent and plainly visible symbol of his work.

The poetry of the last phase covers the poems written within a few years of his death. The most wonderful thing is that in spite of his nervous breakdown and the consequent physical debility neither his mind nor his art suffers decay. On the contrary, he still has his frenzy and his 'eagle mind' as passionate and fantastical as ever. He exhibits full command over his material and writes with perfect ease. With time, he grows more and more distinct and mature in his grip over the complexities of life and world. Growing old among his dreams, he is also conscious of his isolation, his 'lonely aloofness' that is productive. It is the consciousness of this failure to achieve the larger 'unity in life' that gives a peculiar pathos to the epitaph that concludes "Under Ben Bulben" in the last volume of his poems:

> Caste a cold eye
> On life, on death
> Horseman, pass by! (Yeats 208)

"Under Ben Bulben" is his poetic will and testament written in terse lines containing his ideas on history, art and politics. It is in section V of this poem that he writes, "Irish poets, learn your trade,/ Sing whatever is well made" (Yeats 208).

The poetry of W.B. Yeats, thus, has three major classifications—mythological, philosophical or theological, and environmental. Espousing the ideal 'unity of matter and form' in poetry, Yeats, the ardent advocate of culture, custom, grace and aristocratic refinement of taste that together constitute the 'Horn of

Plenty', explores life on different planes of reality and levels of consciousness. The recurrence of the dance rhythm of life in his poems recreates the harmony between body and mind. He considers dance as the supreme embodiment of the union between intellect and emotion. In "Byzantium", "Dying into dance,/ An agony of trance,/ An agony of flame that cannot singe a sleeve" (Yeats 154) denotes the soul's reviewing of all its memories, sins and experiences and its burning in the fire of agony for purgation. Yeats presents the spectacle of purgatory in this burning in the fire of remorse, a fire in the mind. The transmutation of thought into image and soul into body is also a creative journey through Time in his doctrinal poem, "The Phases of the Moon". Robartes says,

> All thought becomes an image and the soul
> Becomes a body: that body and that soul
> Too perfect at the full to lie in a cradle
> Too lonely for the traffic of the world:
> Body and soul cast out and cast away
> Beyond the visible world.

And Aherne corresponds,

> All dreams of the soul
> End in a beautiful man's or woman's body. (Yeats 82)

Through the symbolic journey of the soul round the circle of the year, Yeats explains the philosophy of the phases of the moon. Essentially, a lyric poet with Spenserian energy and coherence in his verse, he fuses passion with thought and makes personal experience impersonal. His poetry, therefore, is both an expression of personality and an escape from personality. Seeking both the intensity of streams and the will of stones, he projects a balanced and liberating vision of life. An outstanding genius of his generation and an accomplished artists, Yeats commands respect for his moral and intellectual excellence. He is unquestionably an ideal poet for all times to come.

Work Cited

Yeats, W.B. *Selected Poetry*. Ed. A. Norman Jeffares. London: Macmillan, 1962. Print.

7

A Note on Yeats's Poetry

Mohan Ramanan

The crux of the writings of Yeats, is that, he should be read for his poetry, for the words and for the rhythms and music, not for the ideas. Indeed at one point of time Yeats believed that words alone are certain good and that living in a world of art was incomparable as a way of life. In this he was in tune with the French Symbolists whose work he learnt and practised. Baudelaire in a poem called "Correspondences" shows how personal neurosis can only be captured by reference to the world of outer nature because nature has a set of correspondences for states of mind and a poet is always turning to nature to evoke the agonies and ecstasies of his heart. Yeats was also part of the Aesthetic Movement of the nineteenth century and he made common cause with poets like Lionel Johnson, Arthur Symons and Ernst Dowson. Symons's "The Symbolist Movement in Literature" influenced him greatly. Also a poet like Blake, who long ago had turned his face away from objective nature and the Newtonian Universe, and intuited truths, which though not orthodox Christianity, had the touch of religious certitude in them, turning the Bible upside down so to speak and arriving at truths which the Church would not accept, but which Man could, had influenced Yeats in no small measure. Yeats also, therefore, turned to mythologies and to a world of the occult, established an elaborate framework of History, not without some help from Vico and Spengler and this cyclic nature of History gave him metaphors for his poetry. The truth value of the system is not the important point—the poetry emerging from it, is. The recurring events and the changes which he thought would occur around 1917 were a necessary part of this Mysticism and Romantic intensity. After all he called himself and his peers the last Romantics. There is truth in this and scholarship shows that much Modernist poetry is Romantic— witness the work of Robert Langbaum, Raehder, Bayley, Kermode and Hough. Bayley speaks of the Romantic Survival, Langbaum of the question of identity and experience and the others have shown how the poets modulated the Wordsworthian egotistical sublime into a well articulated sense of continuity with change where the personal voice the "I" of the poet now got refracted through personae (Pound's title for some of his early poems) and how Yeats attempted to enter the minds of mythological characters to make sense of himself, as did Eliot, who focused on a Prufrock and set up a dialogue between the private and public selves of his character to evoke the despair of a generation. Also most of the Modern Poets had a sense of a time in History when there was a Unified Sensibility and how this had been fractured at some point of time in the past and resulted in a Dissociation of Sensibility. For Yeats it was after the Fall of the Byantine Empire, for Pound it occurred sometime between Petrarch and Cavalcanti and for Eliot it was during the Puritan Interregnum. Kermode and Hough point out that it can't be in the nature of Dissociation to take place at different points of time and they are suspicious that this is actually an invention by the three poets to somehow create the taste for the kind of poetry they wanted to write. Thus, Eliot could write in the Metaphysical mode and effect a convergence between Thought and Feeling. Donne had this capacity and he is opposed to poets who at one point could not feel their Thought or Think their Feelings. Yeats went back to his Irish past and to these improbable myths of history for his bearings. Whatever the truth value of these manoeuvres the point is we have some of the best poems of the twentieth century from Yeats and for that we have to be grateful. Coleridge set up a distinction between the Beautiful and the Agreeable and Yeats's, we have noted, are not always Agreeable but they are always Beautiful.

Scholars have pointed out that Yeats wrote in a Romantic and exuberant style in his early verse. A classic example of this kind of writing is the much anthologized "The Lake Isle of Innisfree" and here we see the escapist Romantic, Yeats, who wants to go away into a happy Townland, to a Never Never land to flee the world which has become too much with him. The atmosphere of escape is visible in the musical cadences of the poems, the rhyme scheme, the diction and the rhythms. It is a haunting poem but it is not the kind of poem he wants to write in future nor the kind of poems he will write in his later phase. We can see the contrast and I shall quote only the opening stanza of the "Lake Isle of Innisfree" and compare it with a short and exquisite poem Yeats wrote later, which is probably a pivotal poem in his oeuvre and indicative of the changes Yeats is going though.

(1) I will arise and go now, and go to Innisfree,
And a small cabin build there, of clay and wattles made:
Nine Bean-rows will I have there, a hive for the honey-bee,
And live alone in the bee-loud Glade.

(2) This is a short poem called "A Coat" from his 1912 Volume significantly entitled *Responsibilities*:

I made my song a coat
Covered with embroideries
Out of old mythologies
From heel to throat;
But the fools caught it,
Wore it in the world's eyes
As though they'd wrought it.
Song, let them take it,
For there's more enterprise
In walking naked.

The contrast between these two poems need not be laboured and the second poem states quite bluntly Yeats's disenchantment with the Celtic Twilight and the need to, as the Imagists might put it, write a poetry of hard, dry, edges. A respect for things combined with finding in it equivalences for mental and emotional states and lifting the significance of things to mythopoeic height—that is Yeats characteristic procedure from now on. It is demonstrated in poem after poem. This resolve is executed in a variety of two ways, but it is broadly Yeats's procedure to go for his materials to where poetry actually resides. He puts it memorably in "The Circus Animal's Desertion":

> Those masterful images because complete
> Grew in pure mind, but out of what began?
> A mound of refuse or the sweepings of a street,
> Old kettles, old bottles, and a broken can,
> Old iron, old bones, old rags, that raving slut
> Who keeps the till. Now that my ladder's gone,
> I must lie down where all ladder's start,
> in the foul rag and bone shop of the heart.

Nothing is intrinsically unpoetic and the job of the poet is to work the materials in such a way as to squeeze out significance from ordinary things or things which hitherto had looked casual and ordinary.

The obvious example of this procedure is "Easter 1916" where Yeats takes up the story of the Irish Republicans who sacrificed their lives for the sake of freedom from the British. It is a classic Yeats poem and contains within itself multitudes. It is in a strict formal framework with a rhyme scheme consistently operating within it, a strict control over diction with nothing out of place in it and with all the trappings of an Imagist poem. But it is more than that. It is what the New Critics would call an inclusive poem because it does not take sides and presents in a balanced way all aspects of the event. This has the effect of both a tension holding the poem up and a structural coherence which lends the poem a classical character, almost Augustan in its propriety and decorum.

Yeats refers to the ordinary way in which Irish people live, moving from counter or desk in government houses and how he has passed them "with a nod of the head".

> Or polite meaningless words,
> Or have lingered awhile and said

Polite meaningless words,
And thought before I had done
Of a mocking tale or a gibe
To please a companion
Around the fire at the club,
Being certain that they and I
But lived where motley is worn. ("Easter 1916")

The casual comedy of Irish life is inclusive of himself and he makes common cause with the rest of his ordinary dull folks. But something has happened to them and to Ireland. "All Changed, changed utterly:/ A terrible beauty is born." The stark statement has the effect of a haunting refrain in the poem and the oxymoron where terrible is conflated with beauty has an uncanny impact on the reader.

What is the nature of this change? Yeats goes on to tell us that a group of Irish patriots have died at the altar of Irish freedom. MacDonagh and MacBride, Connoly and Pearce have been executed for their role in the violent Easter uprising of 1916. This has lifted them to a level higher than anything they had occupied before and has conferred on them almost mythological status. Colonel MacBride was a vainglorious lout and had done much harm to a woman close to his heart (Yeats was thinking of his long time love Maud Gonne whom MacBride had married), Constance Markiewicz had spent her days in ignorant goodwill until her voice grew shrill in the political hustle and bustle, Pearce had been a budding poet and Thomas MacDonagh was coming into his force—all of them had sacrificed their lives creating a beauty in Irish life, long under a casual and numb slumber.

Having numbered them in his song, Yeats asks if they had died unnecessarily because England might have kept faith then all is said and done. Was it needless death after all? The poet expatiates on the nature of sacrifice and the one pointed pursuit of ends so common politics. Hearts with one purpose he says:

Through summer and winter seem
Enchanted to a stone
To trouble the living stream

This image of the stoney-hearted people who sacrificed their lives is further underscored by a beautiful metaphor which Yeats now proceeds to use and here Yeats is at his imagistic best. Here the Image is not a mere Image; it takes on the power of Pound's image as Vortex where energy springs from the Image and energy is poured into it making it no longer a static item but a dynamic symbol:

> The Horse that comes from the road
> The rider, the births that range
> From cloud to tumbling cloud,
> Minute by minute they change;
> A shadow of cloud on the stream
> Changes minute by minute;
> A horse-hoof slides on the brim,
> And a horse plashes within it;
> The long-legged moor-hens dive,
> And hens to moor-cocks call;
> Minute by minute they live:
> The stone's in the midst of all. ("Easter 1916")

The alternating images of change with stability and the rush of things—horses, cocks, hens, water and the presence of the obstructing stone, I believe, centrally captures the paradoxical idea on which the poem is structured. It is the Life within Death paradox. Even as the Irish patriots are showing that they have changed by become violently alive, they breed within themselves the germs of Death. So the Life within Death metaphor is symbolic of the Resurrection of the Irish people, for after all it is Easter the day of Christ's Resurrection. The Patriots get almost a Christ-like status and they move from being ordinary people to becoming mythologically charged.

But Yeats is not done yet. While he bemoans their sacrifice he yet applauds it because as he says he is a poet and his responsibility is to number their names as a "Mother names her child/ when sleep at last has come/ On limbs that had run wild." Enough that they are dead now and have transferred the Nation:

I write it out in a verse—
MacDonagh and MacBride
Connolly and Pearse
Now and in time to be,
Wherever green is worn,
Are Changed, changed utterly;
A terrible beauty is born. ("Easter 1916")

Yeats has immortalized them by according them a status of heroes of Irish myth and legend, not without some religious dimension added onto them for their Easter connection. Thus, Yeats who in his later phase went on to create mythologies, remains a Romantic poet but one who has learnt from the French Symbolists and the English Imagists the value of the Image and the Symbol. He is no longer flying off into the circumambient gas but rooting himself in experience, in life, but in doing so he does not forget that the Self can only be explained in terms of something larger than itself. That is the world of Vision articulated in *The Vision* and the world of Mythologies which give him metaphors for his poetry.

Work Cited

Webb, Timothy, ed. *W.B. Yeats: Selected Poems*. New Delhi: Penguin Books India (P) Ltd., 2000. Print.

8

Politics, Drama and Poetry: The Political Vision of W.B. Yeats as Reflected in Selected "Political" Plays and Poems

Prashant K. Sinha

Several plays of W.B. Yeats have dramatized political issues, especially those embracing Irish nationalism and class conflict including the increasing tension between the native catholic middle class and the landed aristocracy, especially of the protestant variety. *The Countess Cathleen, Cathleen Ni Houlihan* (written in collaboration with Lady Gregory), *The Dreaming of the Bones* and *Purgatory* among other plays are instances of this group. Both Yeats's plays and his politics have been subjected to incisive scrutiny but not the political components in his plays. Peter Ure, one of the seminal critics of Yeats's drama, in his classic study: *Yeats the Playwright: A Commentary on Character and Design in Major Plays*, which takes up all the significant plays with the exception of *Cathleen Ni Houlihan* has no detailed commentary on the political elements in any of these plays. Similarly his essay on "The Plays", i.e. chapter IX of Dennis Donoghue and J.P. Mulrayne's *An Honoured Guest: New Essays on W.B. Yeats* eschews any reference to Yeats's political vision in his drama. Alex Zwerdling in his *Yeats and the Heroic Ideal* dwells upon the nineteenth-century political background in Ireland and Yeats's views on the aristocracy, the middle class and the public life then but he touches upon the political vision in the plays only in a sentence on *The Countess Kathleen*. Daniel T. Torchiana's highly informative study, *W.B. Yeats and Georgian Ireland* provides a detailed analysis of the political issues in *Purgatory*, but it does not examine them in any other play of this kind. In Marjorie Howes edited *The Cambridge Companion to W.B. Yeats*, neither Bernard O'Donoghue in his essay on "Yeats and the Drama" nor Jonathan Allison in "Yeats and Politics" analyzes the political elements in the plays nor Howes herself in "Yeats and the Postcolonial" considers the political vision in them. Alastair D.F. Macrae in *W.B. Yeats: A Literary Life* has a chapter on Yeats and Politics that only has skimpy references to the political elements in the two Cathleen plays.

This paper aims to illuminate the dark political corners in the four above-mentioned political plays. It will also contrast the treatment of political themes in them to that in select poems which articulate similar concerns to highlight what is distinctive as also more shadowy, oblique and peripheral about the dramatization of these issues in the plays. The poems to be considered are "At Galway Races", "September 1913", "Easter 1916", "Nineteen Hundred and Nineteen", "Upon a House Shaken by Land Agitation" and "A Prayer for My Daughter": poems dealing with issues like class distinction, militant resistance to the English, and the Civil War.

Yeats got involved in numerous political activities and controversies even as temperamentally he continued to despise political actions. He never wholeheartedly admired politicians and their profession. In his mind, there was certain ambivalence towards militant nationalism, especially armed rebellion against the English colonial rule. But he was a very self-conscious poet with a persistent awareness of his vocation. On one hand, he had an instinctive inclination to escape through literature into a world of dreams, beauty and romance—it was also a world of old myths and legends—all Irish and therefore in harmony with his patriotic feelings. On the other hand, he also consciously willed himself to accept his "responsibilities" as an Irish nationalist poet, who reflected not only the aspirations but also the lived reality of his country and countrymen. A substantial part of this reality comprised the political developments of his time. This struggle in his self between the desire to escape into a world of fantasy and his political endeavours ironically appears to be more evident in his plays than in his "political" poems.

Ireland has had a tempestuous history since the potato famine of 1840s: starvation deaths were followed not only by large-scale emigration, especially to America but also a political upheaval directed against the colonial masters. Reforms like the disestablishment of the Church of Ireland by Gladstone's Government in 1869, the passage of the First Irish Land Act (1870) and the Second Irish Land Act (1883) did not deter the militant revolutionaries from trying to overthrow the British rule by force of Arms. The Fenians came into existence in 1867, and the Irish Republican Brotherhood arose out of it. It in fact triggered bombings in London in 1883. Parallel to the growth of militant groups was the rise of Charles Stuart (Stewart) Parnell, who tried to secure Home Rule and freedom for Ireland through parliamentary and constitutional means. The fall of this charismatic leader in 1890-91 following the Kitty O'Shea affair and howls of protest from the Catholic clergy and his subsequent death ended this movement. The Home Rule bill which had earlier been defeated in 1886 in the British Parliament fell this time in the House of Lords in 1893.

Soon after Yeats published his first poems and became active in various Dublin circles in the 1880s, he met John O'Leary, a Fenian who had served years in prison and became an exile for opposing the British rule. Yeats came greatly under his spell and said later of himself that he "was a nationalist of the school of O'Leary". Yeats perhaps joined the Irish Republican Brotherhood. His political commitment was further enhanced after he met Maud Gonne, a dedicated activist of Irish nationalism. This young poet had been earlier fired by Shelley's revolutionary lyrical drama *Prometheus Unbound*, and now under these two inspirations, he got actively involved in public affairs. Following O'Leary, Yeats had reservations about Catholics and land agitators, who had organized a fervid rent strike from 1889 to 1891, leading perhaps to the Land Acts of 1903 and 1909. His major public actions in 1890s were his opposition to the celebration of the Diamond Jubilee of Queen Victoria's reign and his leadership of the committee to commemorate the centenary of the United Irish Rebellion of 1798, especially its leader Wolf Tone.

However, following Maud Gonne's disastrous marriage to John MacBride, and four years later, the death of O'Leary, Yeats grew progressively disillusioned with active politics. Nevertheless Yeats's political engagements and reactions took a new turn with the revolutionary capture of the Dublin GPO on Easter, 1916 and the declaration of Irish independence by the leaders of this act. The proclamation of the Irish Free State in 1921 and the Civil War that raged during the next two years between the Free Staters and the Diehard Republicans opposing the partition that is the Black and Tan as against the IRA drew Yeats deeper into politics. In fact, in 1922, he was nominated to the Irish Senate in which he served for six years with distinction.

Nineteen thirties certainly mark a dark phase in the political career of W.B. Yeats. Like D.H. Lawrence, Ezra Pound and T.S. Eliot, he had been an admirer of Mussolini during the early years of the Fascist Government in Italy, but in 1932-33, he took the controversial decision to back the Irish Fascist Blue Shirts led by General Eoin O'Duffy and even wrote the marching song for them. Eventually, he realized his mistake and withdrew his support, but he did not openly denounce them. One instance of his misplaced position regarding totalitarianism came in 1936 when he refused the request of Ethel Mannin, his then lover to nominate for Nobel Prize the German poet in the Nazi concentration camp, Ossietsky. George Orwell expectedly called him a Fascist. His belief in Eugenics also had a parallel in the Nazi espousal of the idea of the superior race. How did the plays and poems relate to his political convictions and stances?

The Countess Cathleen based on the old legend of Countess Kathleen O'Shea, first published in 1892, and revised in 1895, 1901, 1912 and 1923, but first produced in 1899, had as it backdrop the terrible famine of 1847 and also the relief work carried out much later by Maud Gonne who sacrificed much, even her soul according to Yeats among the peasants of Donegal and Mayo facing starvation and eviction. It was really telling that she herself played the role of the Countess when the play was produced. This story of Countess Cathleen distributing her wealth among the starving peasants to save them from the merchants trying to buy their souls, suffering the theft of her remaining money and finally selling her own soul in order to redeem the needy peasants' souls provided Yeats with a fine opportunity to condemn the merchant class and project the landed aristocracy as the caring benevolent guardians of the poor.

In stage directions for scene i, Yeats says "The scene should have the effect of missal painting", thus preventing the total illusion of reality. Moreover, in the early production, Florence Farr played the role of Aleel, the poet, and the very fact that a female was playing a male role must have created further aesthetic distance.

The two men dressed as Eastern merchants, who come to buy souls tell Shemus, their first victim: "We travel for the Master of all Merchants." So Satan is portrayed as the Master merchant in scene i itself. In contrast, Cathleen gives money to the peasants, even emptying her purse after Shemus says: "My curse upon the rich." Zwerdling observes in *Yeats and the Heroic Ideal* that the "middle-class envy and hatred is perfectly brought out in *The Countess Kathleen*" (75). Here the poor as well show this hatred.

In scene ii Cathleen even orders her Steward to

> Sell all I have
> Go barter where you please, but come again
> With herds of cattle and with ships of meal. (38)

In scene iii when the two merchants enter Cathleen's house stealthily and hurriedly and tell her:

> We saw your grain ships lying all becalmed
> In the dark night;

Cathleen censures those

> Who have stored it up
> To prosper on the hunger of the poor. (43)

Thus, she denounces the fundamental capitalistic system of demand and supply. The trading class is shown as going beyond this system to stealing and robbing. Oona, the Nurse rushes in to report:

> The treasure room is broken in.
> The door stands open, and the gold is gone. (45)

Finally, the sale of her own soul represents the supreme sacrifice made by the landed aristocracy to protect and defend the poor peasants. John Lucas points out in *Modern English Poetry from Hardy to Hughes: A Critical Survey* that for Yeats the "ideal Ireland must be that of the gentry and peasantry" with no place for "Middle-class philistinism" (113).

In contrast, poems dealing with the middle class are more explicit in their critique of it. "At Galway Races" in two compact but powerful lines denounced it as the poet referred to the time:

> Before the merchant and the clerk
> Breathed in the world with timid breath.

A later poem "September 1913" makes a frontal attack on the business class as also the devout:

> But fumble in a greasy till
> And add the halfpence to the pence
> And prayer to shivering prayer, until
> You have dried the marrow from the bone;
> For men were born to pray and save: (ll. 2-6)

They are contrasted with the great martyrs in the cause of Irish freedom:

> Little time had they to pray
> For whom the hangman's rope was spun,
> And what, God help us, could they save? (ll. 12-14)

He wonders if it was

> For this that all the blood was shed,
> For this Edward Fitzgerald died,
> And Robert Emmet and Wolf Tone
> And all that delirium of the brave. (ll. 19-22)

So all the sacrifices made by the heroes were wasted on this miserly, timid and devout people. In this poem, Yeats's aristocratic contempt for the calculating bourgeois is quite obvious. Marjorie Howes accurately says in her Introduction to *The Cambridge Companion to W.B. Yeats*: "Increasingly...Yeats's critique of the modern world targeted the middle classes" (7). He has a "special scorn and anger for the middle-class Irish Catholics" (8).

Cathleen Ni Houlihan, written in prose in collaboration with Lady Gregory and produced in 1902 by Maud Gonne's revolutionary group with herself playing the role of Cathleen, is more overtly political than *The Countess Cathleen*. In this work, which distinctly embodies the theme of Irish patriotism, the title itself refers to a symbol of Ireland. Set in 1798 at the time of the French landing on the Irish coast near Killala, it dramatizes how Michael Gillane on the eve of his wedding to Delia Cahel abandons his family and fiancée in order to join in the Irish revolt supported by the French forces against the ruling English colonizers. At the outset, as the family gets ready for the wedding, Patrick, the younger son sees an old woman coming down the road, who is Cathleen ni Houlihan that is Ireland herself. She is "the strange woman that goes though the country whatever time there's war or trouble coming".

As the old woman enters their house and receives shelter there, she complains: "there's many a one that doesn't make me welcome" (80-81). She has no place of her own as the English have occupied it and many Irishmen whose help she sought refused to come to her aid. She has had "too many strangers in the house" (81). She explains: "My land that was taken from me" ..."My four beautiful green fields" alluding to four provinces of the country, i.e. Ulster, Munster, Leinster and Connacht. The old lady makes an overt reference to her friends, to actual historical personage who had suffered or even died for "love of me". They include yellow-haired Donagh who "was hanged in Galway" (82) and others that died "a long time ago". "There was a red man of the O'Donnells from the north, and a man of the O'Sullivans from the south, and there was one Brian that lost his life at Clontarf by the sea, and there were a great many in the west, some that died hundreds of years ago, and there are some that will die to-morrow" (83).

When offered food or drink or silver, the Old woman responds "If any one would give me help he must give me himself, he must give me all" (84)—obviously a stirring call for patriotism. The old woman has "the hope of getting my beautiful fields back again; the hope of putting the strangers out of my house". This hope of throwing the English out of Ireland is based on people both Irish and foreign coming to help her. "I have good friends that will help me. They are gathering to help me now. I am not afraid. If they are put down today, they will get the upper hand to-morrow" (84). The lines also hold out a message of hope that in spite of failures of hundreds of years to drive the English out, the endeavour will succeed one day.

When Michael utters, "I will go with you", the old woman warns him: "It is a hard service they take that help me. Many that are red-cheeked now will be pale-checked and for all that, they will think they are well paid." She continues with her song:

> They shall be remembered for ever,
> They shall be alive for ever,
> They shall be speaking for ever,
> The people shall hear them for ever. (86)

The idea of the immortality of the patriots is sung and thereby the impact is enhanced on account of its sensuous appeal as also its manner of encapsulating the theme succinctly.

As Delia, the fiancée of Michael enters with Patrick, the play shifts from the allegorical to the literal mode. Patrick reports that "There are ships in the Bay; the French are landing at Killala!" He adds: "The boys are all hurrying down the hillside to join the French" (87). Although Michael yields to Delia's request to stay behind and marry her, when he hears the Old Woman singing outside: "They shall be speaking for ever", "he breaks away from Delia and rushes out." The brother reports that the Old Woman has become a young queen. To go back to the Irish legend, Shan Van Voght (Sean Bhean Bhochd: the wretched old woman) has become Cathleen ni Houlihan. Thus, this play is a straight-forward political piece moving from allegory to the literal statement but invariably aiming at giving a stirring call to the Irish audience to rush to action to liberate Ireland from the English yoke. The naturalistic mode of presentation has further contributed to the total immersion of the audience in the immediate action. The use of prose also brings the characters and events closer to real life and leads to more direct involvement of the audience. So in one sense, the play does not explore the complexity of the situation as it gives a somewhat simple-minded battle cry. Perhaps the role of Maud Gonne and her group in the production—in fact of both the Cathleen plays—at least partially accounts for the one-sided nature of the play. As it were, Yeats asked much later in "The Man and the Echo":

> Did that play of mine send out
> Certain men the English shot?

After all, Constance Markievicz is reported, when in prison, to have told her sister Eva: "The play of W.B.'s was a sort of gospel to me."

The Dreaming of the Bones (written 1917) is another play that overtly deals with the Irish resistance in the past. Here Yeats dramatizes the shame and disagree and penance of Dermot MacMurrough and Dervorgilla, two traitors, who betrayed the nation for their personal cause in 1170 and enabled the Normans under Strongbow to become masters of Eastern Ireland. Whereas Michael Gillane had sacrificed his love and marriage for his country, these two sacrificed their country for their love. The play however in set in 1916, and the Young Man, who is the first character to enter, was a part of the uprising at the General Post Office:

> I was at the Post Office and if taken
> I shall be put against a wall and shot. (435)

He puts the shades of the betrayers to an agony of shame as he states that the Irish who sided with the aliens deserved greater condemnation than the enemy soldiers:

> In the late Rising,
> I think there was no man of us but hated
> To fire at soldiers who but did their duty
> And were not of our race, but when a man
> Is born in Ireland and of Irish stock,
> When he takes part against us. (436)

The Young Girl, who is the shade of the female traitor describes the agony they feel on account of their betrayal of Ireland:

> When he has bent his head
> Close to her head, or hand would slip in hand,
> The memory of their crime flows up between
> And drives them apart. (441)

The Young Man immediately knows who these figures were:

> *Young Girl.* Her king and lover
> Was overthrown in battle by her husband,
> And for her sake and for his own, being blind
> And bitter and bitterly in love, he brought
> A foreign army from across the sea.
> *Young Man.* You speak of Diarmuid and Dervorgilla. (442)

The Young Girl concedes the gravity of their crime but pleads

> and yet
> They were not wholly miserable and accursed
> If somebody of their race at least would say,
> 'I have forgiven them'

The young man can only reply:

> O, never, never
> Shall Diarmuid and Dervorgilla be forgiven. (442)

One consequence of their inviting the foreigners to invade the country has been the destruction of the land around this little village that the Young man can see from the summit:

> The enemy has toppled roof and gable,
> And torn the paneling from ancient rooms;
> What generations of old men had known
> Like their own hands, and children wondered at,
> Had boiled a trooper's porridge. (443)

The devastations their action has brought on are so enormous that the sufferings of the guilty seem negligible against it. Yeats moreover uses devices for preventing audience empathy and identification with the characters on either side of the divide. As in another "play for the dancers" like *At the Hawk's Well*, which shows the influence of the Japanese Noh drama, the use of musicians with "their faces made up to resemble masks," employing masks for the shades of the Stranger and the Young Girl, the choice of "any bare place in a room close to the wall" as the stage, a curtain or a screen with a pattern to only symbolize or suggest the scenery, the musicians singing at the time of the folding and unfolding of the cloth all create aesthetic distance and make us more dispassionate when judging and not forgiving the traitors in spite of an awareness of their suffering.

One of the most celebrated poems about Irish patriotism, "Easter 1916" written a few months after the sensational event is a fuller treatment of the theme as it looks at the heroic actions of the leaders of the Easter uprising from more than one angle. At the outset, Yeats depicts them as mediocre, even clownish people. Constance Markievicz, Patrick Pearse, Thomas MacDonagh and John Connolly all led futile and ordinary lives. The poet is especially censorious of John MacBride, "A drunken, vainglorious lout" who

> Had done most bitter wrong
> To some who are near my heart

However, as a result of their heroic action on that eventful day:

> All changed, changed utterly;
> A terrible beauty is born.

This refrain shows how these leaders have become larger than life size. But yet the poet wonders how worthwhile their action was. He asks:

> Was it needless death after all?
> For England may keep faith
> For all that is done and said.

As Marjorie Howes writes in "Yeats and the Postcolonial" this poem "discovers the relative emptiness of claims about revolutionary or decolonizing moments" (217). So Yeats gives us his complex reaction to an action that may glorified as supremely heroic.

Another major poem "Nineteen Hundred and Nineteen" as Norman Jeffares points out in his Notes to Yeats's *Selected Poetry* arose out of Lady Gregory's account of some atrocities committed by both the IRA and Black and Tan. The poet describes the devastations caused by the armed conflict:

> Now days are dragon-ridden, the nightmare
> Rides upon sleep; a drunken soldiery
> Can leave the mother, murdered at her door,
> To crawl in her own blood, and go scot-free. (Section I)

The poet includes in the violence of this "warfare" the lost of "lovely things" and the destruction of artworks and artefacts. He nostalgically recounts with sadness:

> O but we dreamed to mend
> Whatever mischief seemed
> To afflict mankind but now
> That winds of winter blow
> Learn that we were crack-pated when we dreamed.

He complains against the "leveling wind" and tendency to "mock at the great", "mock at the wise", and "mock at the good". In the concluding section of the poem, we go back to "violence upon the roads: violence of horses".

Purgatory, placed at the end of *On the Boiler* (1938), is definitely an elitist play, engaged with the issues of eugenics and the superiority of the aristocracy. The Old Man recalls the past grandeur of the ruined house:

> Great people lived and died in this house
> Magistrates colonels, members of Parliament
> Captains and Governors. (ll. 61-63)

He refers to its desecration when his mother polluted the aristocratic blood by mating with a stable groom. "She should have known he was not her kind." Repudiated by her mother for this act, she died in childbirth. The fact that her husband squandered all her wealth in drinking, whoring and gambling is seen as directly related to his class. Even his act of burning the house down must be seen as a result of his low birth. So must be the felling of the tree. The once green flourishing tree, now stripped bare is symbolic of the decay of the house. As the Old Man says "Fifty years ago", it had

> Green leaves, ripe leaves, leaves thick as butter
> Fat, greasy life. (ll. 22-23)

He states:

> They had loved the tree that he cut down
> To pay what he lost at cards
> Or spent on horses, drink and women. (ll. 69-71)

An uncultured plebian cannot appreciate the "green leaves". The Old Man, the child of this unfortunate union, was not sent to school and grew up as a boorish lout. As a poor pedlar, who at sixteen had killed his wastrel father for burning the house down, he had begotten the "Young Man" upon a tinker's daughter in a ditch" (l. 90). The cycle continues and the Young Son of 16, uneducated and uncultured grows up to be like his father and grandfather—he attempts to rob the former of his moneybag.

It is also significant that the age of the Old Man, when his murdered father and that of the Young worthless son whom he kills at the end is the same as that of the Irish Free State at the time of Yeats's writing of the play—16 in 1938. Is the play at least partially about the failure of the independent Eire? Do the ruined house and the cut tree represent the ruin of the country dominated by merchants and Catholic priests who renounced the great tradition descending from the Protestant Ascendency? Are the Old Man and the Young Son symbolic of two generations of such Irishmen who had destroyed their nation? Their lack of names further encourages an allegorical interpretation. In an interview in *The Irish Independent* (August 13, 1938), Yeats said: "In my play a spirit suffers because of its share in the destruction of an honoured house: that destruction is taking place all over Ireland today." Several Big Houses were burnt down by fanatics in 1922-23.

Anguished concern about the anti-aristocratic trends prevailing in Ireland can also be discerned much earlier in "Upon a House Shaken by the Land Agitation" (1909):

> Mean roof-trees were the sturdier for its fall,
> How should their luck run high enough to reach
> The gifts that govern men, and after these
> To gradual Time's last gift, a written speech
> Wrought of high laughter, loveliness and ease? (ll. 8-12)

Here we have a direct expression of Yeats's belief that equality in any nation or society would mean tangible lowering of levels of culture, refinement and artistic taste which only an elite aristocracy can preserve. It may be rewarding here to recall that in 1902, John Quin had lent him Thomas Common's anthology of Nietzsche's selection. As it were, Herbert Grierson refers to Yeats's interest as a counteractive to the spread of democratic vulgarity.

A decade later after the horrors of not only English-Irish conflicts but also the First World War when he felt "things fall apart", he expressed against in "A Prayer for My Daughter", his unhappiness at the enemies of the existing aristocracy: "Once more the storm is howling" (l. 1) and wondered if the "haystacks and roof-levelling wind,/ Bred on the Atlantic can be stayed" (ll. 5-6). Years of admiration for not only the dwellers of the house at Coole, Lady Gregory and her son Robert, but also her nephews, Captain Shawe-Taylor and Hugh Land had hardened him against all the levelers—the enemies of Great Houses and their rich tradition of culture, taste and courtesy.

From our attempt to examine the plays, not only in terms of their own textures, but also the context of relevant poems, we have seen that *The Countess Cathleen* has a more subduced attack on the merchant middleclass even though the stance is one-sided, than "At Galway Races" and "September 1913", which have more open statements condemning them. The two patriotic plays, *Cathleen Ni Houlihan* and *The Dreaming of the Bones* take a partisan view of the Irish resistance whereas "Easter 1916" is a more complex and multifaceted reaction to a heroic action of a revolutionary patriotic kind. We can say of these two plays: "We make out of our quarrel with others rhetoric," and of "Easter 1916", "but of the quarrel with ourselves poetry". In fact, "Nineteen Hundred and Nineteen" goes beyond them with its gory account of the devastations brought about by the Black and Tan and the IRA during their prolonged armed conflict. *Purgatory* concerned more with class distinction than class-conflict, in a direct and partisan manner extols the traditional aristocracy at the expense of the "lower" or "inferior" classes. The reference to the condition of Ireland, though, is allegorical rather than literal. In comparison, "Upon a House Shaken by Land Agitation" and "A Prayer for My Daughter" make clear but brief and restrained statements against the demand of equality. Thus, the dramatic representations are either partisan or vague and shadowy or both compared to some of the poems. Moreover, these poems deal with the contemporary situations and figures, but the plays are "remote, spiritual and ideal".

To come to the genre related matters, the scope offered by the greater length of the plays leads Yeats to more detailed but not necessarily more comprehensive depiction of the themes. At the same time, factors like stage censorship, popular demands and audience responses also have influenced his work. Could he have said something highly controversial to which the reaction could be as violent as that to *The Playboy of the Western World?* Could he have directly attacked the Catholic Church and faced the kind of ostracism the Sean O'Casey did?

Ultimately, however, we have to go back to his own mental orientation. Perhaps the nature of Yeats's dramatization of political issues in his plays was rooted in a mode of thinking and feeling based on duality, on counterpointing and balancing of opposites: on an interaction of contraries, on a "dialectical process of synthesis," so evident later in his system in *A Vision* and with interesting parallels in earlier and contemporary thinkers as far apart from him as Hegel, the philosopher of history, Jung, the founder of Analytical Psychology and of course William Blake, one of his early inspirations.

Works Cited

Donoghue, Denis and J.P. Mulrayne, ed. *An Honoured Guest: New Essays on W.B. Yeats*. London: Edward Arnold, 1965. Print.

Finneran, Richard J. ed. *The Yeats Reader: A Portable Compendium of Poetry, Drama and Prose*. New York: Scribner, 1997. Print.

Howes, Marjorie and John Kelly, ed. *The Cambridge Companion to W.B. Yeats*. Cambridge: Cambridge University Press, 2008. Print.

Jeffares, A. Norman. ed. *W.B. Yeats: Selected Poetry*. Macmillan, 1962, Calcutta: Rupa, 1992. Print.

Lucas, John. *Modern English Poetry from Hardy to Hughes: A Critical Survey*. London: B.T. Batford, 1986. Print.

Macrae, Alistair D.F. *W.B. Yeats: A Literary Life*. Houndmills, Basingstoke, Hampshire: Macmillan, 1995. Print.

Preface to V.K. Narayan Menon, *The Development of W.B. Yeats* (Edinburgh, 1942) in Alex Zwerdling, *Yeats and the Heroic Ideal*.

Torchiana, Daniel T. *W.B. Yeats and Georgian Ireland*. Evanston: Northwestern University Press, 1966. Print.

Ure, Peter. *Yeats the Playwright: A Commentary on Character and Design in Major Plays*. London: Routledge and Kegan Paul, 1969. Print.

Yeats, W.B. "The Countess Cathleen," *Classic Irish Drama*, Ed. W.A. Armstrong, 1964. Harmondsworth, Middlesex: Penguin Books, 1975.

——. *The Collected Plays*, 2nd edn. 1952. London: Macmillan, 1966.

Zwerdling Alex. *Yeats and the Heroic Ideal*, 1965. London: Peter Owen, 1966. Print.

9

Dhvani Theory and the Poetry of W.B. Yeats

Haladhar Panda

Dhvani theory as elaborated by the ninth-century poetician, Anandavardhana, occupies a significant place in Indian poetics. Associating itself with *Rasa*, the emotion, mood or state of mind and attitude, embodied in a poetic work as *Rasa-Dhvani*, it becomes the key concept in analysing the poem under study and its appreciation. *Dhvani* ordinarily means sound and reverberation in its extensive sense, but as the technical term in poetic theory, it has a variety of meanings. It may mean what is suggested in a poem, or the process of suggestion, or the poem wherein the suggested is the dominant feature. Anandavardhana's definition of poetry: *Kavyastyama dhvani* (*Dhvanyaloka*: 2) uses the body-soul metaphor not only in the definition but repeats the same at different contexts in his treatise. What Anandavardhana means by the metaphor is that *dhvani* is not a constituent of the external structure of *Kavya*; in other words, the body of the poetic work which consists of words and their meaning, the figures of speech, style, and such other elements, and the structure of *Kavya* thus formed is, on the other hand, given significance by the animating principle operating in *Kavya*, designated as *Dhvani* by Anandavardhana through his definition.

Dhvani, meaning suggestion, is wrongly assumed to be the tertiary meaning of expressions after their primary denotative meaning (*abhidha*) and secondary, metaphoric meaning (*laksana*). But *dhvani* is rather what is evoked by both primary and secondary meanings of a text. It is meaningfulness distinguished from all varieties of meanings of a poetic text, a product of the special significative power of resonance or reverberation inherent in poetic language and discovered by the appreciative reader. Anandavardhan observes that the expressed (*vacya*) and the suggested (*vyngya*) have a difference of level in their function: thus whereas the expressed is directly related to the linguistic signs of a text, the suggested is only indirectly related to the same through the significative potency of the expressed. *Dhvani* or *Vyngya* is experienced only through the expressed (*vacya*). Once the expressed is apprehended, there is a sudden flash of the suggested or the evoked. As Abhinavagupta observes: "After the words and their meaning are comprehended, there takes place the sudden apprehension (of the suggested) as directed perception in the mind" (*Abhinavabharati* 279). Because of lack of succession by mediacy and the presence of such sudden leap, the *dhvani* meaning cannot be categorized as either inferred or implied. This is so because the expressed and the suggested form one unit: *vacya* cannot be dispensed with while the *vyngya* is being experienced.

Anandavardhana uses the analogy of lamp-jar relation to clarify the relation between the expressed and the suggested or evoked. In a darkroom, one needs the assistance of the lamp to discover the presence of the jar. This presupposes that the jar is already there in the room and one needs the help of the lamp to reveal the jar to the beholder. Thus, the suggested is what is there with the expressed and the process of suggestion reveals the same not as something entirely new. The second condition inherent in the analogy is that the lamp is to recede to the background and take a subordinate position for revealing the jar in its full glory in perception. Anandavardhana therefore, observes: "That kind of poetry is called *dhvani* by the discerning elders wherein the words or their meaning or both subordinating reveals the poetic signified" (Krishnamoorthy 18). The expressed relegates itself to a subordinate position in order that the suggested be made dominant. The expressed becomes secondary, not in the sense of being useless but it recedes to the background in order to bring the suggested into the foreground and make it dominant. The lamp is not made useless and still continues to shine even after the jar has been illuminated. It is in the very nature of language that it cannot suggest unless it has first expressed. What is expressed in a text thus forms the base for what is suggested. Anandavardhana, therefore, specifies the right condition for the operation of the suggested in a very telling phrase, *samarprana-samartha*, the expressed capable of surrendering its meaning (*vacyartha*) to the suggested (*vyngartha*) intended by the poet.

Anandavardhana categorises the suggested into three types: *Vastu* (idea), *alamkara* (trope) and *rasa* (emotion or mood), but observes that it is the *rasadhvani* or the suggested emotion that is the supreme form of the *dhvani* (suggested) in poetry. Anandavardhana explains that an idea or a trope is generally presented discursively in poetry but when they are not directly expressed but suggested, they are capable of achieving charm and effectiveness. While it is not absolutely necessary for the idea or the trope to be conveyed in the *dhvani*-process, *rasa* cannot be stated like those, it has to be always suggested. Hence, *rasadhvani* or the suggested emotion is, according to Anandavardhana, the 'soul' of poetry. The theory of *rasa dhvani*, thus propounded by Anandavardhana uniting as it does both the formal and contextual factors of a poetic work, is the authoritative formulation of 'literariness' in Indian poetics.

Anandavardhana does not discuss the concept of *rasa* in his treatise but follows the formulation of the same by his predecessor, Bharata. The latter's theory specified that *rasa* arises out of the conjunction of the causes of emotion (*vibhava*), its effects (*anubhava*), and other transient emotions accompanying it (*vyabhicharibhava*). *Vibhavas* are the representations in literature of the actual causes of emotion in life, the characters and the situation in which they are placed: the protagonist being the focus of the emotion and the total situation comprising the scene, antecedent events and other characters in interaction with the hero as exciting the emotion. The effects or manifestations of the emotion are represented in the theatre through speech and gestures of the actors. The basic emotion (*sthayin*) is not mentioned in Bharata's formula, the *rasa sutra*, because it does not actually exist in the theatre: actors can only act its audiovisual effects in relation to the representation of its causes, and the audience can only imagine the same suggested by the actors' performance. On the other hand, the audience in the theatre do not experience the basic emotion as such but not only its transform, the art-emotion or aesthetic experience. *Rasa* thus involves transformation of the emotions of life into their aesthetic configurations which are distinguished from the actual emotions. Hence, *rasa* is always delightful and enjoyable, while the actual emotions may be painful: *rasa* in this 'virtual' and not actual in character in Susanne Langer's characterisation.

Extrapolated from its context of the theatre into that of the poetic work, the *vibhava*, etc. get expressed in language only. Emotion emerges from its correlates descriptively presented in the poem through the process of suggestion in language (*dhvani*). Emotion is thus the suggested meaning of the expressed in poetry and is experienced as *rasa* by the reader. The *vibhava,* etc. being purely linguistic constructs of the actual factors of emotion in life have only an aesthetic or 'virtual' existence. They are neither real nor practical, but idealized: they are neither personal or practical but transpersonalised or universalized: they do not call for action, but only detached contemplation. When the represented correlates of an emotion, thus transpersonalised in poetry impinge upon the said latent emotion in the reader's consciousness, thus conjoined together they give rise to the delectable experience called *rasa*. *Rasa* is thus emotion objectified and transpersonalised, the subject of the reader's disinterested contemplation and is enjoyed as aesthetic experience. The basic emotion (*sthayin*) is the source of *rasa*: it is already there in the reader's consciousness in its latent form, and its correlates represented in the poem simply manifest the same. This is done by the function of suggestion in poetic language and the represented objects in the poem (*vibhava,* etc.) work as the suggestors.

The suggestions, according to Anandavardhana, belong to two levels in a poetic work. The first or lower level consists of items in the linguistic system as phoneme, morpheme, lexeme, and sentence. The second level consists of items in the literary semiotic system where the signifies of the linguistic units of the first level become signifiers at this higher level and are identified as imagery, character, setting, atmosphere, theme and the like. The suggestors are thus sensory objects endowed with the power of evocation. These suggestors can be apprehended by the sensitive reader who is a *sahrdaya*. Thus, *dhvani* gets actualized only in the interaction between the reader and the test. The scope of the text's *dhvani* is conditioned by the relationship of the reader with its language. The poet's expression however powerful for evoking *rasa* is not without limitation. It cannot evoke anything and everything; its suggestive power is limited by the very nature of language; however, its richness depends on the potentiality of the reader. One can isolate to defining characteristics of 'literariness': its figurality or its image-based language; the other its pregnancy or the impliedness of its meaning, both involve the active participation of the reader as *sahrdaya*. The reader's imagination cannot run riot, tied as it is to the evocative power of the poet's language; on the other hand, the reader's sensibility limits the suggestive power of the language of the text. The experience of *rasa* is thus dependent on this two-way traffic between the reader's sensibility and the poet's language and hence, is variable and multiple with regard to the same text. *Rasa* experience in Vardhana's scheme involves, therefore, production of meaning rather than passive recovering of meaning embedded in the text: it is an act on the part of the reader that is dynamically active.

The *rasa-dhvani* theory provides very helpful insights to understand and appreciate the poems of W.B. Yeats, particularly the emotional structure suggested by the poems. *Rasa-dhvani* or the suggested emotion is the meaning of the poem. "No Second Troy" is the most celebrated poem in Yeats's volume: *The Green Helmet and Other Poems*. The poem starts with an explosive question: should the poet blame Maud Gonne, the heroine of the poem, for being responsible for filling his days with misery. This leads to the poet's anger that is directed against the petty violence of the politicians and the activists who would "hurl the little streets upon the great" and fail to appreciate the noble selflessness of Maud Gonne. Thus, both political and personal passion combine in the poem to bestow on it its peculiar power. A comparison with an earlier poem "A Woman Homer Sung"

—reveals how powerful is this later poem in its organization of both structure and texture and its emotion-complex. It is uncertain until the last line of the poem which way the flood of the poet's anger will turn. In the meantime, Maud Gonne is presented in terms of her destructive potential. Her beauty is a tightened bow; her mind is made simple as fire. The image is patently suggestive: it underlines her single-mindedness and uncompromising intensity that is both noble and naïve in terms of the world of practical affairs. The image of the tightened bow further suggests how the heroic beauty cannot help itself being different from the ordinary and should not be blamed for what it is. The series of rhetorical questions following the description create a brilliant piece of dramatic development leading to the final question, the answer of which is hanging in suspense: "Was there another Troy for her to burn?" The theme, motif, the structure and texture of the poem work out a set of complex emotions: of anger, admiration, and critical 'placing' of the heroine's actions at the end. The dominant *rasa-dhvani* of the poem is *raudra*, the furious combined with a submerged note of understanding and compassion for those who cannot help but what they are in reality.

"The Cold Heaven", the next poem to be studied, is one of Yeats's greatest poems and one of the great lyrics in English as well. The poet suddenly turns his eye at the cold heaven which is characteristically ominous in its blend of terror and excitement. The implications of the statement is extended in the image of "burning ice" that underlines in its paradoxical element the tragic preoccupation of the poet with the memory of his hot blood of youth and the burning love that has turned cold with the advancement of his age. The burning ice as an image is potent in its suggestiveness and dramatizes the fact of the poet's burning love that has now turned cold. The dramatic situation in which the poet is placed now highlights for him the wildness of his imagination and heart, wild in their intensity and the havoc they wrought, which now forments him as he is terribly conscious of his present reality, the coldness of age. The casual thoughts of "this and that" at the present moment are discarded by the poet as his mind is driven back to his past. In the meantime, the poet feels conscious of a sense of guilt, "I took all the blame out of all sense and reason"—which is piercingly real for him for not being precisely specified and stated. The next statement of the poet crying and trembling "rocked to and fro" by the passion of guilt leads to the potent image of "riddled with light" where the poet's experience becomes the keenest. Riddled with bullets, the light of the poet's understanding is devastated and he gets confused. Now, his confusion leads to the experience of the death-bed, the turmoil of the physical struggle and the mind's bewilderment as it stares at the unknown, the experience on death. This leads to the image in the final lines of the ghost of the dead lover, naked on the roads, punished by the burning of the cold skies. Individual guilt leads to the terrifying consequence of cosmic punishment meted out by the Heaven in cold indifference to man. The poem thus works out the theme of the coldness and utter indifference of the Heaven with no iota of warmth for the denizens of the earth below it. The complex of emotions underlined in the poem is the complex *rasa-dhvani* as the mixture of the furious (*raudra*) and the terrifying (*bhayanaka*).

"Easter 1916" is one of Yeats's great political poems on the uprising and rebellion of the Irish patriots against the British domination of their motherland. The poem is deeply conscious and troubled by the meaning of heroic action, the implications of which may be different to the observers of that action and sacrifice as their attitudes are varied. The middle-class men who return from their "counter and desk" at the end of their day's work are identified by the exchange of their "polite meaningless" words among one another without any or very superficial involvement. On the other hand, the heroes of the rebellion are in contrast against the "casual comedy" of this "motley" of the unheroic and the average. The poet now numbers among these heroes of the rebellion some among which he first draws our attention to the school master who once was one of "the noisy set/ That martyrs call the world" but is now transformed utterly by his heroic sacrifice in the rebellion. Then the poet remembers one "drunken and vainglorious lout" who had bitterly wronged one very close to the poet's heart. But all of these heroes, whatever they might have been before the rebellion, have undergone a radical transformation through their sacrifice and achieved a deeper life than the casual comedy of ordinary living. The character of this deeper life achieved by the rebels is that their hearts being dominated by the single purpose of rebellion and sacrifice, their minds and hearts have turned "to a stone" which troubles the living stream of ordinary life. In this vital image of the stone in the current of the stream, the poet throws into relief the sudden recognition of the fact that heroic action, however beneficent, by being obsessed is completely a part and parcel of the life that it troubles. While the current of the stream lives minute by minute; the stone as the image of the hearts dominated by the single purpose of heroic sacrifice, continues to trouble the flow. The imagery bestows on the stone its quality of permanence in the midst of change and transience. The lines following work out another implication of the image of stone: "Too long a sacrifice/ can make a stone of the heart." The implication is thus that the stoniness of the rebels' hearts is born out of the tremendous emotional fervour of their sacrifice. The poet, however, is conscious of the implication of his statement the next moment and qualifies the same which otherwise would have turned the rebels' sacrifice to their detriment. He now, therefore, makes another statement hazarding an opinion that it might be that excess of love for their country "bewildered them till they died". Hence, the poet now meditates over the entire event and concludes that not withstanding the very many qualifications of this and that, the event underlines the fact that "A terrible beauty is born" through the heroes' rebellion, valour and sacrifice. The poem is thus a celebration of the *rasadhvani* of the heroic (*vira*).

Although "The Wild Swans at Coole" is a descriptive poem with its photographic realism, it achieves the grandeur and suggestiveness of symbolism. Beginning with the tone of ordinary speech, describing the "nine and fifty swans" floating in the stream, it marks the poet being conscious of his autumnal mood in the "October twilight" setting and with "the woodland paths dry" on which the poet walks. The poet's eyes are now turned towards the contrasted picture of the "brimming water" of the stream on which the swans float and from which they rise to the sky with clamorous brilliance. The swans are now assimilated into the symbolic picture of constancy and unending recurrence set against the inexorable movement of decay. The bell beat of the swans' wings as they rise to the sky which once brought exultation to the poet now rings in the knowledge that a phase of his life, the youthful one, is ending, it brings in with it the sharpness of recognition that is piercingly physical in its impact on the poets. The swans are mysterious in the variety of their suggestiveness. They may stand for the life-force; their hearts do not grow old, they find the streams companionable despite their coldness; passion and conquest attend them unsought, and their vigour is such that they climb the air instead of flying through the same. They may as well stand for inspiration, building by the lake's edge where the wind blows among the reeds. The poet awakes one day into the reality to find them that they have gone away, but he can bring back the dream which they inhabit. All along the suggestion is that the imagination does not age any more than the swans do. The poem is deceptively matter-of-fact, firmly rooted in the landscape of everyday, yet as it unfolds, it achieves the richness and multivalency of the symbolic. The *rasadhvani* registered by the poem is the compassionate or *karuna* for the poet whose emotions move between the past and the present in seamless connectivity.

"The Second Coming" achieves its effect through its archetypal power, going beyond its "thought" into the deeper world of the mythical. Yeats uses the technical term, 'gyre', in the opening of the poem and this is one among a few he resorts to in his other poems; but no special knowledge is called for to understand its sense of the circling and inexorable movement presented in turning and turning in an ever-widening circle. The movement is uncontrollable; the inability of the falcon to hear the falconer dramatizes the loss of contact between the two and highlights the disintegration from the circumference (the falcon) to the centre (the falconer). "Mere anarchy is loosed upon the world" now. With the forces of disorder dominating the scene, the image of the "blood-dimmed tide" potently suggests the fusion of blind passion and apocalyptic violence. The ceremony of innocence being just formal is no resistance against the cataclysmic forces of disorder because the wisdom of the best, the centre of conviction, the basis of moral order has collapsed. The field is open to those who plunge forward on the blood-dimmed tide with "passionate intensity". The ground is thus prepared for an impending revelation, a new annunciation, the second coming. The revelation is ominously vague as the image comes out of *Spiritus Mundi*, its size is vast and troubles the sight because one is unable to comprehend its meaning; the elusive character of the revelation is all the more grim because one is not sure of its implications. The location of this rough beast is in the desert sands; its gaze is described to be blank and pitiless and as it moves its slow thighs, the desert birds reeling away from it in utter giddiness of nightmare cast shadows on the sands. The shape slowly moves to its ferocious actuality; the nightmare gradually comes to life, and the poet wonders as to which "Bethlehem" is going to be its cradle. The universality and immediacy as well as the archetypal and mythical embodiment of the poem's concerns highlight its impressiveness. The poet's feeling is obviously horror as he follows the rough beast coming to the foreground of his observation, but one should not fail to mark the submerged note of fascination behind his dread. What the poem highlights is the poet's awe as well as dread, but it has curiously a note of the sublime. The *rasadhvani* registered by the poem is awesome (*adbhuta*) with an immediacy that keenly pierces the heart of the reader.

The sombre note of "The Second Coming" defines the "great gloom" of the poet in "A Prayer for My Daughter" that follows the earlier poem. The storm of change howls angrily while the poet's child sleeps in a cradle. The "haystack and roof-levelling wind/ Bred on the Atlantic" is only opposed by "Gregory's wood and one bare hill". The storm screams upon the tower, below the arches of the bridge, and the elm trees above the flooded stream. The entire picture highlights the fury of the coming flood. The sea that once gave birth to Venus now threatens a very different birth of the future years, dancing in a frenzy to come out of murderous innocence of the same. In his anxiety and hope, the poet has nothing to do but pray for the safety of his daughter in the midst of this world-devastating storm that is raging all around. The wind bred from the sea's murderous innocence batters not only Gregory's wood but also the "flourishing hidden tree", the ideal image of the daughter's future. The tree is a tree of self-fulfillment, of the inner life around which thoughts cluster like linnets. It further stands for constancy and the life of tradition: it is "like some green laurel/ Rooted in one dear perpetual place". It is likened to "radical" innocence because the storm fails to tear the linnet from the leaf and is thus opposed to the "murderous" innocence of the sea. This innocence is, as the poet imagines, self-contained and an organic expression of the Heaven's will. It finds fulfillment in itself without working against the happiness of others. At the end, the poet states with conviction that it is in custom and ceremony that innocence and beauty are born. The ceremony is the name for the rich horn, the Horn of Plenty, and custom for the spreading laurel tree. The poem is a powerful representation of filial love, *bastalya*, that was later added to Bharata's eight *rasas* by the theorists of poetics.

"Leda and the Swan" is one of Yeats's most famous poems fusing history, myth and vision. The poem uses the sonnet form that is usually employed for celebration of love and public issue. The formal requirements are scrupulously followed except for the break in the eleventh line that is well-judged. The most important characteristic of the poem is its compression: massive themes are pressed into the brief and tightly controlled structure of the poem. Critics have shown that the poem could achieve its richness and power only after several revisions that progressively pruned the inessentials and brought in the compactness and brevity of the poem. The poem begins with the sudden blow of the Swan on the helpless and staggering Leda overpowered by the "great wings" and "dark webs" of the Swan. Leda is stunned by the sudden attack and almost loses her identity under the overpowering force of the bird. The second stanza dramatizes the collapse of Leda's identity through progressive stages by the words: "vague", "feathered", "loosening" and "white rush". The "strange heart" that tightly takes hold of Leda's body at the end of the octave marks the point of crisis. With the ninth line, the consequences of the event so powerfully presented in the octave are examined for comprehension. The sestet now describes these consequences, revealing starkly that violence can be nothing but the fruit of violence, and the overtones of "broken wall" and "burning roof" extends the event's link firmly to the future. The break in the eleventh line referred to earlier now dramatizes the question and examines the issue: when Leda was caught up by the Swan and mastered by his brute force, did she put on his knowledge with power inherent to Zeus as the Swan in the poem before the girl was dropped indifferently by her attacker. The irresistible apocalyptic violence of the Swan has all the savagery of an Annunciation revealed in its power and terror. The source of the tremendous appeal of the poem comes from the combined impact of the *rasadhvanis* of the awesome (*adbhuta*) and terrifying (*bhayanaka*).

"Lapis Lazuli", one of the celebrated Yeats's last poems has the theme of "an act of faith and reason to make us rejoice in the midst of tragedy". The poem was occasioned by the present "of a great piece carved by some Chinese sculptor into a semblance of a mountain, with temple, tress, paths and an ascetic and pupil about to climb the mountain", as the poet wrote to Dorothy Wellesley. "The heroic cry in the midst of despair" is how Yeats described colourfully his undertaking in the poem. The poem, however, wisely moves away from the element of hysteria in the poet's phrasing; the confrontation of tragedy can be endured only when it is aesthetically controlled. "Tragedy wrought to its uttermost"—the suggestiveness of "wrought" drives home the balance of intensity and finesse. The suggestions of "uttermost" are that the dimensions of man's fate have already been compassed by art and the understanding of the same cannot be rendered obsolete. The poet then speaks about Hamlet rambling and Lear raging and all the drop-scenes dropping at once on the stage but without growing by an iota. As the theatre of history unfolds, it goes through the cycle of re-enactments and stresses the aesthetic poise absorbing the destructive and the creative: "All things fall and are built again/ And those that build them are gay." Now history and change are interpreted from the point of view of the work of art. Tragedy does not cease to be tragedy but the tragic experience is soothed into artistic order. As the ascetic and his pupil are seen to climb the mountain carved in the sculpture "Their eyes mid many wrinkles, their eyes,/ Their ancient, glittering eyes are gay." The "mournful melodies" played by the accomplished musician at the bidding of the master, the eyes of the old man amid his many wrinkles—those "ancient, glittering eyes are gay". Thus, gaity is balanced with tragic recognition, life thus asserting itself in triumph against what makes life meaningless. The *rasadhvani* of the poem is *santa*, not enumerated by Bharata is his list of eight, but added by Abhinavagupta while discussing the *rasa* of the great epic, *The Mahabharata*. The informed reader may discover its parallel in Milton's statement at the end of *Samson Agonistes*: "Calm of mind, all passion spent."

The best poems of Yeats, some of which have been analysed and commented upon in the foregoing study, demonstrate not only his involvement but also his sense of creative tension and conflict that dramatise his acute awareness of the alternatives of existence. Yeats writes with passionate recognition of man as the centre of his work. For Yeats, poetic insight takes its birth from inner commitment and conviction; and however stony may be the soil of its strength, the holy tree must always grow in man's heart. Accordingly, he fashions his language to give his insights memorable and vivid expression. The driving force in Yeats's poetry is the assertion of man's creative potentiality. With such concerns in his poetry, Yeats's *ouvre* is one of most humanistic in English poetic tradition.

Works Cited

Abhinavagupta. *Abhinavabharati*. Baroda: 1964. Print.

Anandavardhana. *Dhvanyaloka*, trans. and ed. by K. Krishnamoorthy, Dharward, 1974. Print.

Yeats, W.B. *The Collected Poems of W.B. Yeats*. Macmillan, London: 1950. Print.

10

Reconfiguring the Poet and the Humanist in W.B. Yeats's Poetry

Bijay Kumar Das

Empirical criticism of the nineteenth century takes the biography of the poet as a tool to evaluate his/her poetry. Being subjective criticism, it leaves much to be desired. Subsequently in the twentieth century, there appeared on the critical scene a number of schools of criticism such as New Criticism, Structuralism, Linguistic and Stylistic Criticism, Marxism, Deconstruction, Reader Response Criticism, Feminist Criticism, New Historicism, Postcolonism, Gender Studies, Queer Theory and Eco-criticism in quick succession. Yeats' poetry has been closely studied by numerous critics using one theory or the other. Most of the scholar critics like Richard Ellmann, B. Rajan, A. Norman Jeffares and a few others have analysed Yeats's poetry on the basis of close textual study (Formalist Criticism) by referring to myths and symbols in Yeats's poetry. Stylistics critics and structuralists have studied Yeats's poetry as "Literature as Text", while Reader Response critics have analysed Yeats's poetry from their own standpoint by going to the sources. Edward Said has looked into Yeats's poetry on the basis of postcolonial criticism in "Yeats and Decolonization" (1988). While referring to some of the well-known critics, I would concentrate on the primary sources (i.e., Yeats' poetry) and try to recreate the image of Yeats, the man, the poet and the humanist through his work.

If Yeats is read along with the greatest English poet of the twentieth century, T.S. Eliot, the greatness of the former is revealed. Both Yeats and Eliot used myths and symbols but when the latter's characters are shadowy figures, the former's characters are living human beings drawn from history and contemporary life. Unlike Eliot, Yeats lays emphasis on human love and more so on the consummation of love.

W.B. Yeats's poetry is a world made safe for women. Maud Gonne, Iseult Gonne, Olivia Shakespear, Lady Gregory, Georgie Hyde-Lees, and Helen all appear in his poetry revolving around the poet. They are like 'free play of signifiers' who defy the centre. Sometimes the centre shifts to Maud Gonne, and another time to Lady Gregory or Olivia Shakespear or to Mrs Yeats. Yeats loves them all, as they admire him and love him too. But Yeats dotes upon Maud Gonne, as no poet has done before. Yeats, the man, visualizes the woman, Yeats, the poet, recreates her, "I had never thought to see in a living woman so great beauty" (Jeffares 2001: 172).

I

In my paper an attempt has been made to show how the portrayal of love, death, Irishness, old age, and the predicament of human life in his poetry actually refer to Yeats as a man, who saw life "steadily and saw it whole". The experiences depicted in his poetry is 'the experience felt along the heart', the universalization of human experience springs from his life. I concur with B. Rajan when he says that, "it is unquestionable that Yeats's poetry is, nearly all of it, about himself, it is also unquestionable that it is about a great deal more" (17). Here I am reminded of Yeats's own statement: "A poet writes always of his personal life, in his finest work out of its tragedy, whatever it be, remorse, lost love or mere loneliness, he never speaks directly as to someone at the breakfast table, there is always a phantasmagoria" (Scully 15). Let me begin with Yeats's obsession with Maud Gonne when it comes to his passionate love for a woman. I am inclined to agree with M.L. Rosenthal when he says,

> Virtually every poem celebrating a woman's beauty or addressing a beloved woman has to do with her (Maud Gonne). She is the Helen of his poems, the woman with 'Leadean body', his 'Phoenix' and perhaps 'a sweetheart

> from another life', whose memory embitters his still recent marriage to Georgie Hyde-Lees in the poem, "An Image from a Past Life". (xxx)

Yeats reinforces M.L. Rosenthal's observation in his well-known short poem, "No Second Troy". He asks a rhetorical question:

> With beauty like a tightened bow, a kind
> That is not natural in an age like this,
> Being high and solitary and most stern?
> Why, what could she have done, being what she is?
> Was there another Troy for her to burn? (Webb 64-65).

Yeats implores upon Maud Gonne to return his love, which reminds us of Andrew Marvell's "To His Coy Mistress" (a carpe diem poem). In "When You Are Old", the poet pleads with the beloved to reciprocate his love. He writes:

> How many loved your moments of glad grace,
> And loved your beauty with love false or true.
> But one man loved the pilgrim soul in you,
> And loved the sorrows of your changing face (Webb 30).

Maud Gonne is behind Yeats's idea of beauty, which he could not do without. In "A Prayer for My Daughter", Yeats states unambiguously about it.

> My mind, because the minds that I have loved,
> The sort of beauty that I have approved,
> Prosper but little, has dried up of late (Webb 126).

These lines refer to Yeats's proposal to Maud Gonne and her rejection two times in succession, with a patronizing reply, "Let us go on being close friends" (Jeffares 2001: XVI). Not only with Maud Gonne but also with Olivia Shakespear and Iseult Gonne, Yeats's love, 'dried up'. Marriage to Georgie Hyde-Lees in October 1918 though blossomed, and yet could not heal the wound created by Maud Gonne. Hence, the rhetorical question in "The Tower":

> Does the imagination dwell the most
> Upon the woman won or woman lost? (Webb 132-33).

A thousand Georgie Hyde-Lees could not make a Maud Gonne. Yeats's relation with Maud Gonne remains an enigma. Richard Ellmann's research gives a clue to understand this problem.

> I had always assumed that Yeats remained an unrequited lover, an impression fostered in Maud Gonne's writings. But one day in Dublin, reading an occult journal kept by Yeats in 1908, I came across a passage written late in the year while he was staying with Maud Gonne at Colleville, her house in Norman Countryside. There was an obscure reference to her feeling that they could not continue. I asked Mrs Yeats what was meant and she said, "I wouldn't have volunteered the information, but since you have found it out for yourself, I can confirm that W.B. and Maud Gonne were lovers at that time." (xxvi)

All other subjects and themes pale into insignificance before Maud Gonne. Yeats states it unequivocally in a poem called, "Politics":

> How can I, that girl standing there,
> My attention fix
> On Roman or on Russian
> Or on Spanish politics? (Webb 224).

Yeats's love poetry which began with the idea of the lovers moving together, "My love, we will go, we will go, I and you" ("From the Gaelic"), 'away in the woods' comes a full circle with Yeats's eternal longing to be united with Maud Gonne by recycling life.

> O that I were young again
> And held in my arms ("Politics") (Webb 224).

Now the realization is drawn upon him and the poet states that, "Man is in love and loves what vanishes,/ what more is there to say" ("Nineteen Hundred and Nineteen"). Yeats celebrates himself as the, 'last romantics' and chooses 'Traditional sanctity and loveliness' as his theme. Frank Kermode puts Yeats in the romantic tradition of the nineteenth century.

Kermode makes a valid observation in the following words:

> Poets and artists, says Yeats in *Per Amica Silentia Lunae*, "must go from desire to weariness and so to desire again,

> and live for the moment when vision comes like terrible lightning, in the humility of the brutes". Tormented by the necessary failure of his life, appalled in conscience or in vanity, he can say, "I suffered continual remorse, and only became content when my abstractions had composed themselves into picture and dramatisation." This content is impermanent: the poet is thus perpetually divided against himself. Hence the distinction Yeats makes "between the perfection that is from a man's combat with himself and that which is from a combat with circumstance". Behind it lies the hopeless anger of an artist in love with action, with life. This occupied Yeats incessantly.... (41)

Referring to Kermode, Michael Faherty says that, "Mr Kermode is of course, correct in placing Yeats in this (i.e., romantic) tradition" and then goes on to quote Yeats who said, "we make out of our quarrel with others, rhetoric, but of our quarrel with ourselves poetry" (82).

Yeats celebrates himself as a romantic who 'must be satisfied' with his heart. Hence, he concludes the poem, "A Dialogue of Self and Soul" with an affirmation of life.

> We must laugh and we must sing,
> We are blest by everything,
> Everything we look upon is blest (Webb 164).

If we go by structuralist criticism, we find that Yeats's poetry is exquisitely balanced between the binaries of youth and age, life and art, mortality and immortality. In his Tower Volume of poems there are plenty of such examples. Let us take, "Sailing to Byzantium" for a close analysis. The poem begins with a declarative statement, "That is no country for old man." The word, 'That' indicates Yeats's dissociation from Ireland because here, 'The young/ In one another's arms' is 'caught in that sensual music all neglect/ monuments of unageing intellect'. The old man is out of place in an environment of sensual enjoyment. Yeats likens 'an aged man' to a 'tattered coat upon a stick', not a being but 'a paltry thing'. In order to escape from mortality

Yeats visualizes the holy city of Byzantium where he would invoke the "sages standing in God's holy fire" to guide his soul. Body and soul are shown as binaries in terms of mortality and immortality. Then comes another binary between life and art in the last stanza of the poem. When Yeats wishes to be a golden bird to "set upon a golden bough to sing/ To lords and ladies of Byzantium/ Of what is past, or passing, or to come?"

The paradox inherent in the statement is that man is mortal but art, man's creation is immortal. For Yeats old age, though a course in life, has its impact on the people. In "An Acre of Grass", Yeats writes:

> My temptation is quite,
> Here at life's end...
> Grant me an old man's frenzy
> Myself must. I remake
> Till I am Timon and Lear (Webb 198).

Though old men have been deprived of life's pleasure, their experience is a compensation for this loss in the old age. In "A Prayer for Old Age", Yeats makes it clear.

> God guard me from those thoughts men think
> In the mind alone,
> He that sings a lasting song
> Thinks in a marrow-bone (Webb 189).

Here, a question arises in our mind. Is it correct to say that, Yeats prefers age to youth in his later poetry? Certainly not. Yeats never rejects life and considers old age a curse on humanity. "Among School Children" provides, as it were, an answer to it. When "A sixty-year-old smiling public man" (i.e., Yeats) visited St. Otteran's School in Waterford in February 1926, the image of Maud Gonne is revived in his mind. A. Norman Jeffares makes an apt comment on the development of this poem in *W.B. Yeats: A New Biography*:

> He dreams of Maud telling him of some experience 'That changed some childish day to tragedy'; he wonders if she was like the children he sees:

And thereupon my heart is driven wild:
She stands before me as a living child.

Then he moves to thoughts of her appearance and his, wonders how a youthful mother would feel seeing her child sixty years old. The poem, influenced considerably by the ideas of Gentile, takes off into contemplation of Plato, Aristotle and Pythagoras who became 'Old clothes upon old sticks to scare a bird'. The poem was, he wrote to Olivia Shakespear, a fragment of his last curse on old age; it meant that even the greatest men are 'owls, scarecrows' by the time they achieve fame. The poem's end is a contemplation of life beyond the apparent limitations and restrictions of normal experience, an affirmation of human possibilities (228-29).

While advancing in age Yeats achieved impersonality in art. It is Yeats who in the words of T.S. Eliot, "out of intense and personal experience, is able to express a general truth, retaining all the particularity of his experience to make of it a general symbol" (Cullingford 76).

"A foolish, passionate (old) man" of "A Prayer for Old Age" becomes a wise old man in "Why should not Old Men be Mad" who realized life on life's terms. Hence, comes an apt observation:

Some think it a matter of course that chance
Should starve good men and bad advance (Webb 207).

When young men are oblivious of it, old men feel it in their pulses.

II

Having discussed Yeats as a poet of love, old age and above all a romantic, let me turn to other aspects of Yeats as an Irish poet, postcolonial poet, humanist, who has been 'the consciousness of an age' (Eliot's Coinage) (Cullingford 80).

Yeats longed to be an Irish poet writing for Ireland. It was the old Fenian leader, John O'Leary who inspired Yeats to write for Ireland and be an Irish poet. Maud Gonne came to Yeats's house with a letter from O'Leary for John Butler Yeats. Yeats fell in love with her at first sight, and tried to impress her by writing love poems.

As A.N. Jeffares writes in *The Circus Animals*:

> ...his love for Maud became inter-twined in his hopes for Ireland; was she not the living embodiment of beauty and did she not represent the person of Ireland, all the young grace and old wisdom of Cathleen ni Houlihan? She turned his attention from dreaming of a heroic age to the everyday realities, some of them, it must be admitted, fantastic enough, of revolutionary politics (11).

He makes a case for Ireland in "Under Ben Bulben" in the following lines:

> Many times man lives and dies
> Between his two eternities,
> That of race and that of soul,
> And ancient Ireland knew it all (Webb 209).

In the same poem, Yeats implores upon other Irish poets to write about Ireland.

> Irish poets, learn your trade,
> Sing whatever is well made (Webb 211).

Though Yeats began as an Irish poet, he outgrew that level and became an English poet, the same way the American Eliot became an English poet. In *The Identity of Yeats*, Richard Ellmann makes a valid observation on this point in the following words:

> He is Irish, he is also anti-Irish in an Irishway, and his interest in Irishman is always subordinated to an interest in man.... Ireland is his symbol for the world and he is caught between estrangement and love for both (4-5).

Edward Said seeks to describe Yeats both as a colonial and postcolonial poet in his essay, "Yeats and Decolonization" included in his book, *Culture and Imperialism*. The idea of bringing knowledge and power to be juxtaposed against violence is characteristically Yeatsian. The Irish colonial era prompts him to examine the violence associated with it. Said writes:

> In the Irish colonial setting, Yeats seems best able to pose and re-pose the question provocatively, using his poetry, Blackmur says, as a technique of trouble. And he goes further in the great poems of summation and vision like

> "Among School Children," "The Tower," "A Prayer for My Daughter," "Under Ben Bulben," and "The Circus Animals' Desertion". These are poems of genealogy and recapitulation, of course: telling and retelling the story of his life from early nationalist turbulence to the status of a senator walking through a classroom and thinking of how Leda figured in all their pasts, or a loving father thinking about his child, or a senior artist trying to achieve equanimity of vision, or finally, as a long-time craftsman somehow surviving the loss (desertion) of his powers, Yeats reconstructs his own life poetically as an epitome of the national life (Bayoumi and Rubin 311).

Since Yeats divided his time between Dublin and London, he was never anti-British in his attitude to life and poetry. British poets were his favourites and therefore, "his poetry began by echoing Shelley and Spenser and the pre-Raphaelites" (Jeffares XIII). I think Yeats was oblivious of colonization and therefore, he was not concerned with Irish/British conflict. Poetry is his passion and therefore, he never felt the pinch of colonization. I think, Edward Said's argument inherent in the passage quoted earlier in this paper, seems to be misplaced.

Yeats himself clarifies his position in his essay, "A General Introduction for My Work" in the following words:

> Then I remind myself that though mine is the first English marriage I know of in the direct line, all my family names are English, and that I owe my soul to Shakespeare, to Spenser and to Blake, perhaps to William Morris, and to the English language in which I think, speak, and write, that everything I love has come to me through English; my hatred tortures me with love, my love with hate (Scully 22).

Yeats writes with Ireland in his bones but discovers it only through English. Yeats shuttled between Dublin and London frequently. The intellectual in him discarded the political, as Norman Jeffares states in *W.B. Yeats: A New Biography* in the following words:

> Maud Gonne's letters and his own accounts tell the significant story of how he was horrified by the Jubilee

> Riots in Dublin in 1897. He was exhausted by his political work and near a breakdown, from which he recovered after a spell in Sligo and his first long summer as Lady Gregory's guest at Coole Park in Country Galway. He left the IRB in 1900, probably as a result of having seen political violence in action three years earlier, as well as experiencing disgust at the IRB's failure to deal effectively with Frank Huge O'Donnell (xiv).

Edward Said's brand of postcolonialism hardly suits Yeats, though his apt observation, "William Butler Yeats has now been almost completely assimilated into the canon as well as into the discourses of English literature and European high modernism holds good" (Bayoumix and Rubin 292). He can be compared to only one poet in England, that is, T.S. Eliot. He has few peers but not many equals in English literature. Like Eliot, Yeats sees life as incomplete and his resolution, 'Myself must I remake' is not dissimilar to Eliot's determination, 'shall I set my lands in order'?

I think B. Rajan's assessment of W.B. Yeats as a poet along with T.S. Eliot is very apt and incisive. Yeats may lack Eliot's humility, but

> ...in Yeats, unlike some of his contemporary colleagues, it is not merely the intellect which is at the tips of the senses but, surprisingly and excitingly, the senses also. Most important, Yeats is the supreme poet of what an earlier century would have called the passions; it is through these passions, worked upon by the organising power of poetic language, that Yeats is able to enter the centre of conflict which is man and to re-create that conflict as the substance of poetry (Rajan 192).

Yeats's universality and integrity as a poet lie in his humanity and insight into human nature. He has outgrown his declared stand, "to write for my own race/ And the reality" in "The Fisherman". In "Sailing to Byzantium" he implores the sages, "Standing in God's holy fire" to, "consume my heart away, sick with desire" for "it knows not what it is, and gather me/ Into the artifice of eternity". In speaking for himself Yeats speaks for humanity in general for we do not know ourselves and blunder our way into oblivion. Yeats has gone a long way from "The Living men that I hate/ The deadman that I loved" to "Those that I fight I do not hate/ Those that I guard I do not love" in "An Irish Airman Foresees his Death" which transcends time and place across centuries. Bhisma and Drona in *The Mahabharata* best exemplify Yeats's ideas behind the line, for they never hated the Pandavas against whom they fought and never loved the Kauravas whom they guarded. In the end Yeats, the man and Yeats, the poet are welded together, who himself is the unity of his work.

Works Cited

Bayoumi, Mustafe and Andrew Rubin. *The Edward Said Reader*. New York: Vintage Books, 2000. Print.

Cullingford, Elizabeth, ed. *Yeats: Poems, 1919-1935*. London: Macmillan Press Ltd., 1984. Print.

Eliot, T.S. "The Development of Yeats" (1940). *Yeats: Poems, 1991-1935*. Ed. Elizabeth Cullingford. London: Macmillan Press Ltd., 1984. Print.

Ellmann, Richard. *The Identity of Yeats*. London: Faber and Faber Ltd., 1964; rpt. 1968. Print.

——. *Yeats: The Man and the Masks*. Oxford: Oxford University Press, 1979. Print.

Faherty, Michael, ed. *The Poetry of W.B. Yeats*. New York: Palgrave Macmillan, 2005. Print.

Jeffares, A. Norman. *The Circus Animals: Essays on W.B. Yeats*. London: Macmillan and Co. Ltd., 1970. Print.

——. *W.B. Yeats: A New Biography*. London: Continuum, 2001. Print.

Kermode, Frank. *Romantic Image*. Fontana: Collins, 1971. Print.

Rajan, B. *W.B. Yeats*. London: Hutchinson and Co. Ltd., 1965; rpt. 1972. Print.

Rosenthal, M.L., ed. with "Introduction". *Selected Poems of William Butler Yeats*. New York: The MacMillan Company, 1962, Print.

Scully, James, ed. *Modern Poets on Modern Poetry*. London: Fontana, 1977. Print.

Webb, Timothy, ed. *W.B. Yeats: Selected Poems*. London: Penguin Books, 1991. Print.

11

The Personal and the Impersonal: Yeats Versus Eliot

Rajnath

Yeats and Eliot are the two major poets of the twentieth century and both have evolved their critical concepts out of their experiences as poets. Both emphasize the simultaneous presence of the personal and the impersonal in poetry. Yeats moves from the personal to the universal while Eliot depersonalizes his personal experience.

Yeats frequently employs terms that point to the extremes that he wishes to eschew such as sentimentalist/rhetorician, anarchic subjectivity/naturalistic objectivity. Distinguishing between the rhetorician and the sentimentalist, Yeats writes in 'Ego Dominum Tuus':

> The rhetorician would deceive his neighbours,
> The sentimentalist himself, while art
> Is but a vision of reality.

The rhetorician is a propagandist who employs his resources of language to impress and thereby deceive others, while the sentimentalist is deceived by his own illusions. In his essay "Anima Hominis", Yeats further elaborates, on the distinction between the rhetorician and the sentimentalist saying that the former is interested in his public image, while the latter in his

---

This is a revised version of the essay "Yeats, Eliot and Personality/Impersonality" which first appeared in *Critical Essays*. Ed. S. Vishwanathan et al. (Madras: Macmillan India, 1987).

private happiness stemming from things like money, position, and marriage. Similarly, the anarchic subjectivist is too much concerned with himself as against the naturalist whose concern is external reality. Thus, neither of these attains that 'vision of reality' which goes into the creation of true art.

Having rejected the extremes, Yeats posits the co-presence of opposites. Describing the tragic conception in his *Autobiography* he says categorically that 'no mind can engender till divided into two' and goes on to demonstrate through the examples of Keats, Shelley, and Synge the intellectual and emotional aspects of the mind. And in his essay on "Anima Hominis" he remarks that "we make out of the quarrel with others, rhetoric, but of the quarrel with ourselves, poetry". Whatever meaning we give to the word 'quarrel', it certainly implies some kind of dialectic. But Yeats has made more direct pronouncements on the dialectical nature of a work of art. In his "Poetry and Tradition", he states that "the nobleness of the arts is *in the mingling of contraries*, the extremity of sorrow, the extremity of joy, perfection of personality, the perfection of its surrender..., and its red rose opens...at the trysting place of mortal and immortal, time and eternity" (*Essays and Introductions* 255) (italics mine). It is evident that for a work of art there is no question of either/or; both the terms of the dialectic are essential for its existence. Yeats elaborates further the dialectic of personality and the surrender of personality in his *Autobiography* where he writes:

> Does not all art come when a nature, that never ceases to judge itself, exhausts personal emotion in action or desire so completely that something impersonal, something that has nothing to do with action or desire, suddenly starts into its place, something which is as unforeseen, as completely organized, even as unique, as the images that come before the mind between sleeping and waking (255).

What Yeats is driving at is that the poet does not describe his immediate personal emotion with its roots in action or desire but subjects it to cogitation and through cogitation discovers some impersonal ideas. He is of the opinion that a poem written out of direct personal emotion will be but a bad poem. It is on this ground that he dismisses the War poets who, he thinks, "were too near their subject matter to do...work of permanent importance" (*Essays and Introduction* 500). In his "General Introduction for My Work" Yeats distinguishes between the trivialities of the poet's personal life and the universal, i.e., impersonal idea into which he is reborn, and in his *Autobiography* describes poetic genius as "a crisis that joins buried self" (226) for certain moments to our trivial daily mind. The 'buried self' or the 'memoried self', as Yeats calls it elsewhere, is the same as Jung's collective unconscious which the 'trivial daily mind' of the individual partakes of. Thus, the poem becomes a dialectic of the personal quotidian self and the impersonal 'buried self'.

Like Yeats, Eliot also emphasizes the dialectic of personality and impersonality in poetry. Throughout his critical programmes, Eliot suggests that in poetry personality and impersonality meet in one form or another. "Tradition and the Individual Talent" is essentially a dialectic of personality and impersonality. As the personal talent comes into contact with the impersonal literary tradition, both affect each other and undergo mutations: tradition gets individualized and the individual talent gets 'traditionalized'. If the poem has no contact with tradition or is a mere repetition or imitation of tradition, it is doomed to failure. At one extreme, the poem will be too personal, while at the other it will be too impersonal. Eliot envisages the interaction of tradition and the individual talent when he says: "It is a judgment, a comparison in which two things are measured by each other. To confirm merely would be for the new work not really to confirm at all: it would not be new and would therefore not be a work of art" (*Selected Essays* 5).

Eliot says time and again that it is only a poet with personality who can be impersonal in the true sense. Towards the end of "Tradition and the Individual Talent" he writes:

> Poetry is not a turning loose of emotion, but an escape from emotion, it is not an expression of personality, but an escape from personality. But, of course, only those

> who have personality and emotions know what it means to want to escape from these things (*Selected Essays* 21).

Apparently, Eliot does not deny the importance of the poet's personality but then what is the exact relationship between the personality and the poem? In his essay on "Shakespeare and the Stoicism of Seneca", Eliot says that Dante and Shakespeare have transformed their personal agonies into something universal and impersonal. Of Shakespeare he writes:

> Shakespeare, too, was occupied with the struggle—which alone constitutes life for a poet—to transmute his personal and private agonies into something rich and strange, something universal and impersonal (*Selected Essays* 137).

The poet evidently transmutes his personal experience into something universal and impersonal, but the question arises whether personality as such gets into the poem.

In fact, Eliot does not deny that personality does get into the poem but we get from him two different versions of personality. Personality is the day-to-day life of the poet, his quotidian self and personality is also what Tillyard calls 'mental pattern' (35). In his early phase Eliot, unlike Yeats, argues that it is only personality as mental pattern or what Eliot calls 'point of view' that gets into the poem, while all the trivialities of his daily existence are left out. In his essay, "Humanist, Artist, Scientist" (1919), Eliot writes contrasting the humanist with the artist and the scientist: "in the man of scientific or artistic temper the personality is distilled into the work, it loses its incidents, it becomes, as with Montaigne, a permanent 'point of view', a phase in the history of mind" (*The Athenaeam* 1015). It is this emphasis on point of view and de-emphasis on what Eliot calls elsewhere 'particular events in...life' that account for pronouncements like "the progress of an artist is a continual self-sacrifice, a continual extinction of personality" (*Selected Essays* 17) and "the more perfect the artist the more completely separate in him will be the man who suffers and the mind which creates" (*Selected Essays* 18). The personality in these statements is the poet's life, not his mental pattern or point of view.

In his later phase Eliot, like Yeats, believes that the personal experience of the poet, i.e., the experience of the particular events in his life, does get into his poetry, but it must widen into something impersonal. Of Paul Valery's *Le Serpent* he writes: "It is 'impersonal' in the sense that personal emotion, personal experience, is extended and completed into something impersonal—not in the sense of something divorced from personal experience and passion" (14). And he makes the same point more emphatically in his essay on "Yeats" (1941) where he says contrasting the impersonality of a mere craftsman with that he finds in Yeats: "The second impersonality is that of the poet who, out of intense and personal experience, is able to express a general truth, retaining all the particularity of his experience to make of it a general symbol" (*On Poetry and Poets* 255). Eliot even realizes that he is contradicting his earlier stance on impersonality. What Eliot calls 'impersonal' or 'general' here is the same point of view which he calls personal in his early phase. But the contradiction lies in the fact that in his early essays be insisted on the exclusion from the poem of the personal experience in the sense of the particular events in life, while in his later phase he pleads for its inclusion.

Though Yeats and Eliot are essentially in accord on the dialectic of the personal and the impersonal, they differ on the nature and significance of philosophical poetry. Yeats wants the poem to necessarily start at the personal end and hence fails to appreciate those poems where the starting point is an impersonal philosophical system or religious orthodoxy. In his essay on "Modern Poetry", Yeats is sympathetic towards philosophical poems like T.S. Eliot's *The Waste Land* and Herbert Read's *Mutations of the Phoenix* where philosophy is not the philosophical system of a particular philosopher but more or less fabricated by the poet himself out of odds and ends; he fails to appreciate "the young communist poets who complicate their short lyrics with difficult metaphysics" (*Essays and Introduction* 52). In the same essay, he arraigns communist poetry as 'impersonal philosophical poetry' and praises the Irish poets by saying that "instead of turning to impersonal philosophy they [the Irish poets] have hardened and deepened their personalities" (*Essays and Introduction* 52). Yeats gives the impression that communist poetry, or any poetry, for that matter, starting at the impersonal end, can never be good. But, in point of fact, poetry starting at either the personal or the impersonal end can be good or bad. If the poet can sufficiently personalize the impersonal philosophy (whether Communist or Christian) he can certainly write good poetry depending on his technical virtuosity. The possibility of such a poetry has been fully realized by Eliot in *Four Quartets*.

Unlike Yeats, Eliot believes that good philosophical poetry is possible only where the philosophy is derived from the philosopher and not fabricated by the poet himself. He censures Blake for fabricating his own philosophy and praises Dante and Donne for using philosophical ideas formulated by others. As he writes in *Shakespeare and the Stoicism of Seneca*, "The poet who 'thinks' is merely the poet who can express the emotional equivalent of thought" (*Selected Essays* 135). And of Donne he writes in his unpublished "Clark Lectures": "Donne was able to find the emotional equivalent of highly abstract, or generalized ideas" (143). The 'emotional equivalent' is, in fact, the personal equivalent, because it is inevitable that the emotional is the emotion of the poet. Thus, Eliot envisages a poetry where the poet offers us the personal equivalent of an impersonal philosophical system, the kind of poetry that has been written by Dante and Donne. This poetry will be the converse of the poetry idealized by Eliot in his early phase, where the poet depersonalizes his personal emotion.

Though the same dialectic of personality and impersonality has been emphasized by both Eliot and Yeats, Yeats errs on the side of personality, while Eliot errs on the side of impersonality. Consequently, Yeats cannot envisage poetry starting at the impersonal end, while Eliot can think of poetry as completely, impersonal. Yeats's error has been examined above. In his "Tradition and the Individual Talent", Eliot holds that in respect of depersonalization "art may be said to approach the condition of science" (*Selected Essays* 17) and goes on to employ a chemical analogy to describe how the poet's mind operates in artistic creation. He says that when oxygen and sulphur dioxide come into contact with platinum, they form sulphurous acid, though the platinum itself remains unaffected and the new gas contains no traces of platinum. Platinum in this analogy is the mind of the poet and sulphurous acid, the new gas, is the poem. At another place in the same essay he remarks that "the poet has not a 'personality' to express, but a particular medium, which is only a medium and not a personality, in which impressions and experiences combine in peculiar and unexpected ways" (*Selected Essays* 19-20). Here Eliot is flatly denying that the poet has a personality to express not realizing that by his own argument personality as point of view is always present in poetry.

The difference between Yeats and Eliot can be best construed in relation to their poetry. Yeats best poems usually start off with the poet's personal experience which is widened into something impersonal or universal. His 'Among School Children' is an instance in point. The poet visits a school as a 'public man' and finds himself in the midst of school children. The presence of the school-girls reminds him of the childhood of the woman, presumably Maud Gonne, he himself was passionately in love with. But now the poet begins to reach for the universal archetype embodied in the school girls, Maud Gonne as well as Helen, the daughter of Leda and the Swan. And the old age of Maud Gonne, and by extension, of any woman, raises the question of appearance and reality, becoming and being and the poet's mind goes back to Plato, Aristotle, and Pythagoras who speculated on this question. What one finds in the poem is the impersonal archetype emerging from the poet's personal experience. This is what Yeats implies by the co-existence of 'trivial daily mind' and the 'buried' or 'memoried' self.

As against Yeats, Eliot in his early poetry tends to leave out of his poetry his quotidian existence. He gives us the archetypes which are expressed in the particulars remote from the poet's personal life. A recent interpretation of *The Waste Land* treats the poem as analogous to Tennyson's *In Memoriam* expressing the poet's personal grief occasioned by the loss of his young friend, Jean Verdenal, who dies in action during the First World War. John Peter's, "A New Interpretation of *The Waste Land*" (1952), "With Postscript" (1969), *Essays in Criticism*, 19 (April 1969), and James E. Miller's has elaboration of Peter's interpretation in his *T.S. Eliot's Personal Waste Land* (Chicago: The University of Chicago Press, 1978) reinforces the analogy between *The Waste Land* and *In Memoriam*. This may or may not be true, but we have it on the poet's own testimony that the poem expresses "a personal and wholly insignificant grouse against life" (qtd. in Valerie Eliot 1). But nowhere in the poem does the poet appear in his own person. The poet's personal experience is expressed only by implication. What Eliot has done is to use the objective correlative derived from Miss Weston's *From Ritual to Romance* and other sources to formulate his personal feeling. The only personal element that one can locate in the poem is the poet's point of view, but for the rest one has to go into the life of the poet. Unlike Eliot's, Yeats's personal life is present in the poem.

The second type of poetry that Eliot has idealized, especially in his later phase, he himself has attempted in the *Four Quartets*. Here Eliot starts at the impersonal end and moves into his personal life. Christian orthodoxy which is impersonal in the sense that it is shared by all Christians is lent a personal form. Whatever philosophy one discerns in the poem is not the poet's own fabrication but derived from philosophers like St. Augustine, Bergson, and Bradley. In order to personalize what is already impersonal, the poet at times appears in his own person, for example in the lines starting with "So, here I am, in the middle way, having had twenty years,..." Moreover, the titles of the four quartets have the personal associations of the poet. Eliot stayed in "Burnt Norton", a large country house, in 1934; "East Coker" is named after the ancestral village of the poet; "The Dry Salvages" is a group of rocks off the coast of Cape Ann where Eliot spent his boyhood and 'Little Gidding' is named after a small country church that Eliot himself had visited.

The Waste Land starts at the personal end, while the *Four Quartets* starts at the impersonal end, but both display the same dialectic of the personal and the impersonal. The particular events of the poet's life are left out of *The Waste Land*, while in the *Four Quartets* they are part of the poem. This explains why in his later phase Eliot believes that the particularity of the poet's experience must be retained.

Eliot has been generally acknowledged as a major ctitic but Yeats as a critic has not been accorded the same status. However, Yeats's critical postulates help in understanding his own poetry as well as poetry in general. A comparative study of the two poet-critics sheds significant light on the difference in the nature of their poetry.

Works Cited

Eliot, T.S. *Selected Essays*. London: Faber and Faber Ltd., 1951. Print.

——. "A Brief Introduction to the Method of Paul Valery". *Le Serpent Par Paul Valery*. Trans. Mark Wardle. London: Cobden Sabderson, 1924. Print.

——. "Clark Lecturs on the Metaphysical Poetry of the Seventeenth Century". *John Hayward Bequest*. King's College, Cambridge (quoted with the permission of Mrs Valerie Eliot). Print.

Yeats, W.B. Essays and Introductions. New York: Macmillan, 1961. Print.

——. *Autobiography*. New York: Collier Books, 1968. Print.

——. *On Poetry and Poets*. London: Faber and Faber, 1969. Print.

——. "Anima Hominis". *Mythologies*. New York: Collier Books, 1980. Print.

Tillyard. *The Personal Heresy*. London: OUP, 1965. Print.

Montaigne. *The Athenaeum*. 10 October 1919. Print.

Select Bibliography

Bloom, Harold. *Yeats*. Oxford: Oxford University Press, 1970. Print.

Cullingford, Elizabeth, ed. *Yeats: Poems 1919-1935*. London: MacMillan Press Ltd., 1984. Print.

Desai, R.W. *Yeats's Shakespeare*. Evenston: North Western University Press, 1971. Print.

Donoghue, Denis and J.R. Mulryne, ed. *An Honoured Guest*. London: Edward Arnold Publishers Ltd., 1965. Print.

Ellmann, Richard. *The Identity of Yeats*. London: Faber and Faber Ltd., 1964; rpt. 1968. Print.

——. *Yeats: The Man and the Masks*. Oxford: Oxford University Press, 1979. Print.

Faherty, Michael, ed. *The Poetry of W.B. Yeats*. New York: Palgrave MacMillan, 2005. Print.

Henn, T.R. *The Lonely Tower: Studies in the Poetry of W.B. Yeats*. London: Methuen, 1965. Print.

Jeffares, A. Norman. *W.B. Yeats, Man and Poet*. London: Routledge and Kegan Paul, 1949. Print.

——. *The Circus Animals: Essays on W.B. Yeats*. London: MacMillan and Co. Ltd., 1970. Print.

——. *W.B. Yeats: A New Biography*. London: Continnum, 2001. Print.

——. *A New Commentary on the Poems of W.B. Yeats*. London: MacMillan, 1984. Print.

Kermode, Frank. *Romantic Image*. Fontana: Collins, 1971. Print.

Kirby, Sheelah. *The Yeats Country*. Dublin: Dolmen Press, 1962. Print.

Leavis, F.R. *New Bearings in English Poetry*. Harmondsworth: Penguin Books, Ltd., 1967. Print.

MacNeice, Louis. *The Poetry of W.B. Yeats*. London: Oxford University Press, 1941. Print.

Malone, A.E. *The Irish Theatre*. London: Constable, 1929. Print.

O'Donnell, William. *The Poetry of William Butler Yeats: An Introduction*. New York: Ungar, 1986. Print.

Pinto, V. de S. *Crisis in English Poetry 1880-1940*. London: Hutchinson and Co. Ltd., 1951; rpt. 1967. Print.

Rajan, B. *W.B. Yeats*. London: Hotchinson and Co. Ltd., 1965 rpt. 1972. Print.

Rosenthal, M.L., ed. *Selected Poems of William Butler Yeats*. New York: The MacMillan Company, 1962. Print.

Scully, James, ed. *Modern Poets on Modern Poetry*. London: Fontana, 1977. Print.

Stead, C.K. *The New Poetic: Yeats to Eliot*. London: Hutchinson, 1964. Print.

——. *Pound, Yeats, Eliot and the Modernist Movement*. London: MacMillan, 1986. Print.

Stock, A.G. *W.B. Yeats, His Poetry and Thought*. Cambridge: Cambridge University Press, 1961. Print.

Tindall, William. *W.B. Yeats*. New York: Columbia University Press, 1966. Print.

Thuente, Mary Helen. *W.B. Yeats and Irish Folklore*, Dublin: Gill and MacMillan, 1980. Print.

Unterecker, John, ed. *Yeats: Collection of Critical Essays*. N.J. Prentice-Hall, Inc., 1963. Print.

——. *A Reader's Guide to William Butler Yeats*. London: Thamers and Hudson, 1959. Print.

Ure, Peter. *Yeats, the Playwright*. London: Routledge and Kegan Paul, 1963. Print.

Webb, Timothy. W.B. Yeats: Selected Poems. New Delhi: Penguin Books India (P) Ltd., 2000. Print.

Index

A

Allison, Jonathan, 74

Anandavardhana, 89-92

Auden, W.H., 1

B

Babbitt, Irving, 33

Baudelaire, Charles, 56, 66

Bharata, 91

Blake, William, 33, 57-59, 87

Blavatsky, Madam, 27, 32, 56

Bloom, Harold, 1

Brown, Terence, 1

C

Chatterjee, Mohini, 27, 57

Common, Thomas, 86

D

Das, Bijay Kumar, 4

Desai, R.W., 3

Donne, Jonn, 67

Dowson, Ernst, 66

E

Eliot, T.S., 1, 24, 33, 56, 61, 63, 67, 102-03, 111, 117, 121

Ellmann, Richard, 1, 3, 7, 102, 105, 109

Emerson, 10

F

Farr, Florence, 77, 106

Fitzgerald, Edward, 78

G

Gonne, Maud, 2-4, 6, 11, 14-16, 43-48, 50, 52-54, 56, 61-62, 70, 76, 79, 81, 93, 103-05, 108

Gonne, Iseult, 103

Gregory, Lady, 12, 56, 73, 79, 84, 86, 103

Gregory, Robert, 86

H

Harding, Walter, 14

Hegel, 87

Henn, T.R., 1

Hyde, Douglas, 10
Hyde-Lees, Georgie, 104-05

I

Indra, C.T., 4
Isherwood, Christopher, 36

J

Jefares, Norman A., 1, 44, 84, 107
Jones, Burne, 56
Jung, C.J., 87

K

Keats, John, 57-58
Kermode, Frank, 1, 54, 67, 105-06
Kinsella, Thomas, 1
Krishnamoorthy, K., 90

L

Langbaum, Robert, 67
Lawrence, D.H., 76
Leavis, F.R., 1
Lucas, John, 78

M

MacBride, John, 11-13, 14, 44, 70, 76, 83
MacDonagh, Thomas, 70, 83
Malachuk, Daniel S., 21
Mallarme, 59
Mannin, Ethel, 76
Marlowe, Christopher, 50
Markievicz, Constance, 81, 83
Marvell, Andrew, 104
Merriman, Brian, 24
Morris, William, 56
Mulrayne, J.P., 73

N

Nelson, Howard, 13-14

O

O'Donoghue, Bernard, 74
O'Leary, John, 56, 60, 75, 108

P

Panda, Haladhar, 4
Pater, Walter, 59
Pound, Ezra, 1, 48, 56, 63

Q

Quin, John, 86

R

Rajan, B., 1
Rajnath, 4
Ramaswamy, S., 4
Reine, Kathreen, 35
Rosenthal, M.LO., 103-04
Rossetti, D.G. 57
Russell, George, 36, 56

S

Said, Edward, 1-2, 102
Sewall, Ellen, 13-15
Sexton, Melissa, 11
Shakespeare, William, 3, 30-34, 46, 55
Shelley, P.B., 57
Singh, Prabhat K., 4
Sinha, Prasanta, K., 4
Spengler, 66
Starkie, Walter, 35
Stead, C.K., 1, 49
Stevenson, R.L. 56
Swami, Prabhavananda, 37
Swami, Sri Purohit, 28-29, 37, 80
Symons, Arthur, 56, 66

T

Tagore, Rabindranath, 1

Tennyson, Lord Alfred, 57

Thoreau, Henry David, 3, 7, 9-17, 21-24

Tynan, Katharine, 10, 16

U

Ure, Peter, 73

V

V. Vico, 66

Viswanathan, S., 4

W

Whitman, Walt, 7, 10, 17

Y

Yeats, W.B., 1-7, 10-13, 15-23, 27, 29, 31-34, 36, 38-44, 56-57, 62-72, 74, 78, 94, 103, 106-07, 118-19

Z

Zwerdling, Alex, 73